The Bridge

The Bridge

Behind the Scenes at Chelsea

JON NICHOLSON & OLIVER HOLT

BOXTREE

First published 1998 by Boxtree

an imprint of Macmillan Publishers Ltd
25 Eccleston Place, London SW1W 9NF
and Basingstoke

Associated companies throughout the world

ISBN 0 7522 2424 7

Photographs copyright © Jon Nicholson 1998
Text copyright © Oliver Holt 1998

1 3 5 7 9 8 6 4 2

A CIP catalogue record for this book is available from
the British Library.

Printed and bound in Great Britain by
The Bath Press plc, Bath

Reproduction by
Speedscan Ltd.

Contents

The Team

TEN MILES FROM CENTRAL LONDON, inside the M25 but outside the cluttered pages of the A-to-Z, the flight paths of the planes winging into Heathrow Airport point the way to the innocuous cluster of college playing fields and the two-storey red-brick pavilion where they have been filling in the gaps of every Chelsea season for the past eighteen years.

If Stamford Bridge clasps the heart of the club, its soul lies out here in the uninspiring countryside on the fringes of the capital. The public ecstasies and agonies of the club may be played out in front of 35,000 people at a stadium that has rapidly become an entertainment empire with its megastore, hotel and restaurants, but to the players and the coaching staff, Harlington is more like home.

This is where it happens. This is training, the glamour-free part of football, the part where the game is stripped to its essentials, where there is no crowd and no hiding place, where a modern Premiership club with all its multifarious commercial interests is peeled away like the casing around a nut, exposing the kernel at the centre, a group of men playing football alone and unhindered, pounding themselves daily into the ground. It is like a training camp for gladiators.

Down here is where the tactics that can shape a season are thrashed out, where the planning and the post-mortems are held, where the injured repair for treatment, where Gianfranco Zola practises his free-kicks and the players eat and bathe. It is here where dreams of making the first-team squad are granted or dashed on a weekly basis, when a sheet is pinned up on the notice board and the names of those who have been omitted are scored through with black ink.

It is here too, behind the scenes, where much of the power within the club resides. If Chelsea's chairman, Ken Bates, and his right-hand man, Colin Hutchinson, cradle much of it in their plush offices in the village that has grown up around the football club on Fulham Road, the influence wielded by the tight-knit group of coaches, administrators and physios – hardened, honest, football men – who work at Harlington should not be under-estimated. Ruud Gullit found that out to his cost. Significantly, it was in the manager's small office at Harlington where Hutchinson began to tell Gullit the news that his services were no longer required.

The training ground, with its pitches, its canteen, its changing rooms, showers and gymnasium, is a melting pot, a magnet for visiting players and teams. One week in early December, Rosenborg, the Norwegian champions, trained there to prepare for their Champions League match with Real Madrid because Norway had become too cold. On another day, Frank Rijkaard, Gullit's former AC Milan teammate, arrived to take his Dutch coaching badge with his old friend.

For a club that paved the way for the post-Bosman move towards polyglot teams in the FA Carling Premiership, chock-full of exotic foreign imports, wonderful talents such as Zola, the new boss, Gianluca Vialli, Roberto Di Matteo and Gullit, stars whose skills we once only admired open-mouthed on television, there is something entirely apt about the positioning of their training ground so close to the country's traditional entry point for travellers. It is like the Ellis Island of the new nation that is English football.

When they fly in from brief trips home to see their families, a car spirits them to Harlington in ten minutes. Sometimes, Frank Steer, one of the club stewards, goes to pick them up or runs them out there when they go on a visit home. Its location was one of the main reasons in persuading Mark Hughes

Early morning at Harlington: the supporters gather as training begins.

The boot room: scrubbed clean by the YTS boys, the boots hang in neat lines under the initials of each player.

to sign for Chelsea from Manchester United in the summer of 1995 because he was determined his family home should remain in the north west. 'If I had had a long drive at the end of the plane journey, I could not have got away with it,' he says.

At the north end of the group of pitches, a ground owned by London University's Imperial College and leased by Chelsea for the past eighteen years, cars crawl past on the M4 at one of its worst trouble spots, just before Heathrow and the exit to the M25. The Italian players drive to work this way from their homes in Kensington, looking for the landmark of the concrete mass of the Forte Hotel to tell them it is time to exit the motorway. They negotiate the roundabout, head for Sipson and know they are nearly there when they see the great semi-circle of poplars towering over the flat, characterless terrain.

They drive in here in their BMWs, their Mercedes and their Porsches between 9.45 and 10.15 a.m., depending on whether or not they want breakfast. They park in the spaces that are reserved for them and sidle up to an unassuming side door that opens on to a corridor at the back of the pavilion. They nod their greetings to the regulars, people such as Frank, a club steward for twenty-seven years, Gary Staker, another steward who speaks fluent Italian and helps to chaperone Vialli, Zola and Di Matteo, and Felicity Harris, a middle-aged woman who is in care but leaves her residential home at 7.30 a.m. two mornings a week to come to see her idols.

One corridor runs the length of the pavilion. It has a slight kink in the middle at the point where a set of double doors opens out on to the training pitches. At one end is the gym with its isokinetic machine for measuring the muscle strength of players recovering from injury, its weights machines and exercise bikes. The massage room is at that end,

too, and the office where the chief physio, Mike Banks, assesses injuries.

Next to the physio's room is a door marked 'Manager's Office'. Gwyn Williams sits in here. He has been with the club for eighteen years, taken on by former manager Geoff Hurst, and has filled just about every position in the hierarchy. Youth development officer, reserve team manager, chief scout; he has done it all. His title is Assistant Manager now but it would in fact be more accurate to call him the general manager.

He is at the very hub of the club, the one who organises travel, puts up the team sheets, tells the players their duties and bosses around the youth-team lads. A no-nonsense figure with a manner that can be brusque when he doesn't know or trust somebody, when he wants to hurry things along, he is also the conduit for the press, the man everyone has to go through to set up an interview with any of the players. Nothing happens at Harlington without his knowing about it. Underestimate his influence at your peril.

The boot room, where Bob 'Oz' Orsborn the kit man, sits surrounded by 300 pairs of boots decorated with all sorts of bright stripes and puts kit after kit into metal suitcases for away trips, is across the corridor, an Aladdin's Cave of footwear where the boots are arranged vertically. At the top are a player's initials and under each GV or GLS there are six pairs of boots, all the same brand but with differing numbers of studs and stud depth for different weathers.

That is the staff end. On the other side of the kink, it is the territory of the players. The members of the first-team squad are the kings here. They are the loudest, they have an extra spring to their strut, an added confidence to their manner. It is unspoken but the rest defer to them as young schoolboys would to their elders. Like school, peer groups seem to split

The corridor at Harlington where young hopefuls rub shoulders with heroes such as Gianfranco Zola.

horizontally. The first-team players chat mainly to each other, the reserves do the same.

Gradually, as more and more of the homegrown younger players, youths such as Nick Crittenden, Mark Nicholls and Paul Hughes, progress towards the first team as they began to do last year, the integration may change as it has done at Manchester United, where the younger boys have flooded into the team.

Still, it is to Chelsea's credit that there are no cliques within the group, none of the divisions among the first-team squad that seem to be rife elsewhere, none of the jealousy or mistrust of the foreigners that is rumoured to boil under the surface at clubs such as Arsenal and Sheffield Wednesday. At Chelsea, perhaps because the Italian contingent, in particular, works so hard, because Zola and Di Matteo are so unassuming and Vialli is proving himself such an enlightened player-manager, they are among the most popular of all the personnel.

It is a macho atmosphere in there, a bit like an army barracks, exclusively male and echoing with shouting and raucous laughter. It smells of liniments like Deep Heat and before the players run out on to the pitches it resounds with the noise of studs on the hard floor mixed in with yells of encouragement and micky-taking.

The first-team players usually change in the two rectangular rooms at the end of the corridor furthest away from the staff offices. One is occupied by the younger players, men such as Michael Duberry, Jody Morris, Paul Hughes and Frank Sinclair, the ones who call themselves the 'rebels'. The other is home to the more established professionals, players like Mark Hughes, Frank Leboeuf and Graeme Le Saux.

Next to them, there are three other rooms, generally favoured by the reserves and the fourteen younger players who are attached to Chelsea via the government's Youth Training Scheme. Most of them pad around in various states of undress. Duberry, the club's England Under-21 centre back, favours a white dressing gown with the words 'The Enforcer' scrawled in black capital letters on its back.

Across the corridor from the changing rooms are the shower rooms where the players head straight after training and which quickly turn into a source of billowing steam. There are six individual baths in there, too, a great sunken communal bath and some scales. Next to the showers and the baths, there is a separate room with toilet cubicles and a couple of urinals.

There are other offices even further down the corridor, mainly used by the groundsman, Mick Reynolds, but Chelsea personnel hardly ever venture that way. If they go through the double doors, it is usually to climb the flight of stairs to the canteen for breakfast or lunch or to head to a room right at the back of the first floor of the pavilion, where the press gather every Friday after training to talk to Gullit, earlier in the season, and later Vialli, and a couple of selected players about the match that lies ahead on Saturday or Sunday.

The canteen, which looks like any school kitchen, with its shiny metal food bar at the front and its stove and pots and pans at the back, is run by Sian Bowles. Before she was brought in by Glenn Hoddle, Gullit's predecessor, three years ago, many of the players used to head back towards Stamford Bridge for lunch and eat in the Lost Café, a glorified snack bar on Fulham Road, about 100 yards from Fulham Broadway tube station.

Now, most of them head upstairs. If they want breakfast, usually cereal or toast, they have to arrive by 9.45 a.m. Most of them are conventional eaters but one or two flaunt their idiosyncrasies. Frank Leboeuf, the tall, bald, fresh-faced Frenchman who is

Duberry's central defensive partner and one of the most elegant players in the Premiership, draws yells of disgust when he indulges his favourite habit of pouring coffee over his cornflakes and tucking in with gusto. It sets him up, he says, for the exertions ahead.

TRAINING USUALLY STARTS AT ABOUT 10.45 although it is put back sometimes if the traffic is particularly bad on the M4 or the M25, a concession to one of the great modern-day ills. The youth-team players are almost always the first out. Some of them are routinely kicking a ball around near the pavilion by 10 a.m. but these are the ones who have had to come in early to lay out the senior players' kit.

The goalkeepers – and there were four of them at Chelsea during the 97/98 season – have their own coach, Eddie Niedzwiecki, one of the most talented goalkeepers the club had ever had until his career was cut short by injury. They usually train alone, perhaps with someone from the reserves drafted in to give them shot-stopping practice. The reserves are taken by Mick McGiven, the youth team by Ted Dale.

When the first team run out, they are passed first of all into the hands of Ade Mafe, the British former sprinter who was appointed as Fitness Coach soon after Gullit took over at Stamford Bridge three years ago. Mafe also helps injured players in the middle stages of their rehabilitation but his first task every day is to warm the players up for training.

He needs about twenty minutes to half an hour, he says, to get them ready. They jog a couple of times round the pitches first and then concentrate on general mobilisation exercises, lots of stretching and some sprints to warm up the muscles. The players separate off into little groups as they jog, chatting to each other, slapping each other playfully round the head, catching up. Mafe says that Dennis Wise, the club captain, is the fittest player at the club. 'It is

effort and ability and outstanding application,' he says. Over ten yards, Andy Myers, a defender who had his short-cropped hair bleached blonde for the whole of the 97/98 season, is the fastest sprinter, pressed closely by Zola. Over fifty metres, it is Duberry or the young left-back, Danny Granville, who joined Leeds United at the end of the 1997/98 season. 'Anything beyond fifty metres is Michael Duberry territory,' Mafe says.

Duberry is a young man who wears his heart on his sleeve. Some say he is a young Ian Wright in temperament, the soul of any party, exuberant, hot tempered and prone to depression when things go wrong. Upstairs in the canteen, Sian says he is their favourite. He's the joker in the team, the one who pretends to grab their handbags and sprinkles sugar in their hair. 'He drives us mad,' Sian says. 'But he's not very good in the mornings.' Always bringing up the rear in the first slow morning jog around the pitch, Duberry looks as though he can hardly drag his huge frame round the ground as he labours along behind the rest, in his sweat-top and his blue bobble hat pulled down right to his eyebrows. One morning in particular at the close of last year, he looked particularly out of sorts.

The previous night at Carrow Road in Norwich, Duberry had played in an England Under-21 match against Greece. The match, the second leg of a tie that England had to win to qualify for the European Under-21 championships, was widely seen as a fine opportunity for young men such as Duberry, Liverpool's Michael Owen and Leicester City's Emile Heskey to advance their claims to be included in Glenn Hoddle's England squad for the World Cup finals in France.

Heskey scored twice, Owen once but Duberry had a disappointing game in the match which sealed England's exit. He was blamed for the first goal and admitted he had suffered a lapse in concentration. At half-time, he apologised to the rest of the team for it. At the end of the match, he stalked off the pitch looking like thunder.

When he arrived at Harlington the next morning, his mood had not improved. He stomped around the corridor. Frank Sinclair, the club's right-back, asked him how it had gone and said he had only seen highlights of the game. 'It was shit,' Duberry said. 'Absolutely shit.' As he walked out on to the pitch, Graham Rix, the first-team coach, greeted him almost too cheerily, as if he knew what kind of response he was going to get. 'All right Doobs?' he said. 'All right,' Duberry muttered.

By the time he had dragged himself outside, the rest of the first team had already completed their jog and were gathered in a circle a hundred yards away. Duberry set off on his own, jogging painfully slowly as if he was weighed down by the agony of a missed opportunity. As he ran, it was as if his mind was transparent, as if everyone knew his thoughts. In his head, he was thinking he had blown it, that after all the battles he had had against injury, he had fallen again just when his goal had hove into view.

Nobody teased him much that day because they could sense his deep depression. They could also sense, perhaps, that he was in a menacing mood. But training is a merciless place for jokes and wind-ups: the Monday after England had squeezed a 0–0 draw against Italy in Rome last October to seal their own automatic qualification for the World Cup but consign the Italians to the play-offs, Zola and Di Matteo arrived at Harlington to find special t-shirts had been made to commemorate the occasion.

On the front, they said 'England on tour – France 98'. On the back, there was a more simple legend. 'Italy?', it said. Zola and Di Matteo could hardly complain, though. The day after their victory over

England at Wembley in February, they had arrived at Harlington wearing their national team shirts.

After Mafe has finished with them, the first team begin working with the ball. When Gullit was in charge, he used to oversee these sessions with Rix but since Vialli took over midway through February, more responsibility passed to the coach because Vialli was always out on the pitch with his playing hat on. The reserves play on another pitch, watched over by McGiven. What they concentrate on depends on what day of the week it is and how quickly the next fixture is approaching.

In this age when Sky television and the commercial slavery of Uefa have made a mockery of the traditional routine of playing matches on Saturdays and Wednesdays, there is no such thing as a normal training week for Chelsea. Involvement in the European Cup Winners' Cup, played on Thursdays during the 97/98 season so it did not clash with Uefa Cup matches on Tuesdays or Champions League matches on Wednesdays, played havoc with any attempt to establish a semblance of a routine. The general principle, though, is that if the team plays on Saturday, the players get Sunday off. If there is no midweek match, they get Wednesday off, the day, coincidentally, that Imperial College use the ground during the week.

Working within that model, Monday is usually a gentle, general training day spent partly shaking off the stiffness of the weekend and analysing the match before. On Tuesday, the player-manager will take a normal session in the morning, break for lunch and then take the first team out again in the afternoon for a harder, more intensive session. Five years ago in England, training in the afternoons would have been unheard of but the influence of foreign managers such as Vialli, Gullit and Arsene Wenger at Arsenal and the peripatetic Roy Hodgson at Blackburn Rovers has changed that now.

Eddie Niedzwiecki, the goalkeeping coach, puts Frode Grodas through his paces.

Ade Mafe prepares to warm up the players at Harlington.

Zola, Clarke and Di Matteo enjoy themselves despite the rain during a sodden training session.

With Wednesday as a day off, Thursday becomes the crucial day, the day when things turn serious, the joshing stops and a real element of competition is added to the mix.

'Thursday is normally the day when they begin to concentrate on the pattern of play,' Williams says. 'Luca talks about how we are going to play and how they are going to play against us and that is the time when you start sorting the men out from the boys. They have a match among themselves and the ones who get bibs to wear over their shirts are the ones who know they are not going to be playing on Saturday. The others are going to work hard to try to prove to the manager that he is wrong, that they should not have been left out and the ones who are in have got to prove that they deserve it. Friday is the day when you organise your set plays. There is a short and sweet five-a-side, some short sprints and then that is it: time for action.'

Some aspects of training changed when Vialli took over. Immediately, there was more hard, physical work, more running, the kind of fitness training that will benefit the players in the future. With Vialli immersed in playing, the role of Rix also became much more prominent.

'I think the lads have responded very positively to Luca in training,' Rix says. 'Whenever a new manager takes over there is always that little push, that little impetus, I don't know, but you have to maintain it. I think they have responded well in the different training regime that he wanted. It is more physical, more structured and we actually do work on things whereas before, Rudi's attitude rightly or wrongly was "well, we've got the best players, we'll go out and play". But you still have to be very organised and work at certain things.

'We do more shadow play, unopposed, now, sow the seeds in people's heads. Shadow play is when you set a team out. You don't even need a ball and there will be no opposition. I would have the ball and I would say "I'm Ryan Giggs of Manchester United, I've got the ball here, where should our team be according to that?". Then I would say, "Now I'm David Beckham, now I'm Gary Pallister" and wherever I am on the pitch we will stop it and have a look at the shape of the team. Then we will do it offensively with a ball. It will be to show midfield men where they could be making runs as a ball is laid back.

'Luca joins in every day. Because of injuries and age, that wasn't always the case with Rudi so Rudi would be on the side with me and he would say what he had to say. Whereas Luca, because he is playing every day, we discuss beforehand what he wants and then he just leaves it up to me, totally.

'Even before a match, if we have a three o'clock kick-off, then by twelve he has told me what he wants, the team, where we are going to press and then he says "from now on I am a player". I have to give a team talk before the game, portray the tactics to the players. Rudi did all that. At half-time, I go in and do the talk even when Luca is not playing. He doesn't only ask me. He asks the players and the other members of staff. He is trying to glean what he can off players. Rudi would just come in and say "right, this is what we're doing".

'I feel like I am earning my money now. Rudi gave me a certain amount of stick after he left because he said "all Graham Rix did at training was referee games". That was only because that was all he wanted me to do. Vialli is asking questions of the players, the medical staff, Ade Mafe, me and trying to get the best out of everybody, push them to extremes, which if you want to get the best out of people you have got to do.'

THOSE WHO HAVE A DREAMY VIEW OF TRAINING as some sort of tactical think-tank, though, where the opposition are destroyed on the drawing board before a ball is kicked, where players work constantly on out-manoeuvring their opponents with their formation or their approach, have got it wrong. 'We have so many games during the season,' Rix says, 'that most of the time it is just a case of keeping the boys ticking over. We do not get a lot of time to practise things. We just want to make sure that the lads enjoy it and have a laugh. The tactics and all that come pre-season. We lay down certain rules that we want to carry on through the season then. During the season, it is just a matter of reminding them. Little reminders all the time.

'In training, it is really about their pride. Most of those lads go out in training and they want to be the best player. It is their pride and their ego that drives them on. They work hard. They are a good set of lads and because of the system we have, they never really know who is going to play. They see people like Zola staying behind after training to practise his free-kicks and they know that if he can do it, anyone can do it.' He is right about the pride, too. When a game starts out on those pitches, any game, a five-a-side, a full-blown match, a game of head tennis over a volleyball net slung up on the far side of the furthest pitch, pulses quicken and expressions set. Suddenly, those players could be anywhere. They forget themselves, forget that the M4 is a few hundred yards away and that nobody is watching, and immerse themselves in the spirit of competition that is partly responsible for getting them to this level in the first place.

The cries of elation and anguish when goals are scored or missed are exaggerated in this environment, perhaps, and may not carry quite the same adrenaline rush as a goal in a Premiership match but there is a sense of triumph and despair about each one just the same. It is here, at training, when you realise with relief that the pressures and the huge incomes notwithstanding, these are men who love their jobs, who live for playing football.

Paradoxically, the time it struck home most, was when the eye strayed to the reserves, playing a full-scale, up-tempo match on a pitch adjoining the one where the first-team squad were training. There were all sorts of players on that pitch, young hopefuls with their careers ahead of them, hopeful, brash and thrusting, and old pros whose glory years are behind them and who had no chance of breaking into Gullit's star-spangled plans. One of the latter was David Rocastle, who won two league titles with Arsenal and fourteen England caps. Since he joined Chelsea in the summer of 1994, he has played just twenty-seven league games for the first team and last season he was not even within sniffing distance, never in the first-team squad, let alone on the substitutes' bench.

On this particular day in training, when winter had come and the sky was as grey as slate, the morning was nearly over but still Rocastle, who moved to a Malaysian club near the end of last season, was trying for all he was worth in this training game that meant nothing and could not lead to his promotion to any higher level. He fought and cajoled to the end, though, and just as McGiven shaped to blow his whistle, Rocastle created one last shooting opportunity for himself. He shot low and hard but the years have dulled his aim and he dragged his effort wide of the right-hand post. A look of horror spread over his face, he let out a cry and then fell to the floor as much in exhaustion as disappointment. The whistle blew, the rest traipsed past him and into the changing rooms and still he lay there. For a while he was still, contemplating another small failure, then he hauled himself to his feet and walked in, too.

No pain, no gain: in the Harlington gym,
Gianluca Vialli stretches his muscles before
a training session.

WHILE THE PLAYERS ARE OUT ON THE PITCH, the pavilion is a hive of activity as the support staff go to work. By the double doors that look out on to the pitches, stewards Frank and Gary stand for a while, watching the first team, shooting the breeze, swapping stories about the antics of Felicity, warding away unwanted visitors and getting balls, calendars and posters ready for the players to sign when they come back in.

Out on the pitches, Felicity stands behind one of the goals where the first team are playing, a hood pulled over her head to protect her against the cold, watching intently. After a while, she trudges forty or fifty yards away and begins kicking a few stray balls back towards the pitch whence they have come. After training has finished, she hangs around by the players' door until the last one has left and then she begins the long journey home. She is fifty-two, she says, although she looks older, and she has been living in care since her mother died last year. At Christmas, a card from her was the only one pinned up on the Harlington notice board. She goes to all the weekend games, home and away. Her favourite player now is Di Matteo although Leboeuf, as amicable a player as you get, routinely puts his arms round her when she waits inside the double doors. She has even been known to give a team talk to the first eleven after a special request to Rixie, who calls her Phyllis. She has been going to watch Chelsea train for twenty-seven years now.

It started when the club training ground was near her home in Mitcham. 'I was hooked then,' she says. And when they moved to Harlington, she kept coming. Now she leaves the home at 7.45 a.m. to start her journey. She walks to the local station and catches a train to Wimbledon. From there, she gets on the Piccadilly Line to Hatton Cross and then a bus to within half a mile of the ground. She walks the rest. Her surname is Harris. 'You're related to Ron Harris, then,' I say. 'Unfortunately not,' she says.

Behind the barriers, in term-time as well as in the holidays, there is always a small gaggle of schoolgirls standing in the cold making the kind of lewd remarks that schoolgirls do, discussing which of the younger players they fancy most and generally trying to engage Frank in a bit of banter. 'Have you got a plastic bag?' one of them shouts over to him. 'Why? Have your knickers gone?' he says.

'I love it here,' Frank says one day. He travels up from Brixton four days a week, gets to the training ground before the gates open, waits around for ten or fifteen minutes and then goes in when they are opened up. He used to be a London bus driver but got retired on medical grounds. He's rotund now – some of them call him 'Fat Frank' affectionately – but he puts the signs out in the morning that warn the punters that it is strictly players and officials only beyond a certain point, and he occasionally turns his hand to washing off the boots of the young sons of some of the players who come down to kick a ball about in the holidays and then he chats with whoever rolls up.

Like Gary and Felicity, he's part of the fabric of the club. It is to the credit of men such as Gwyn Williams that they recognise his worth and reward his loyalty. On one level, what he does is menial, almost irrelevant, on another it helps things tick over and emphasises there is still room for a bit of character, history and substance in a club that is fast becoming a huge one-team industry to rival any in Britain.

Rix often stands there with them, too, by the tap where the YTS boys douse the boots and teases them as they work in the intervals when he is not racked by an habitual hacking cough. Sometimes he has a white plastic chair brought out for him to sit on while he drinks a coffee.

Felicity, one of the Harlington regulars, waits for the players to emerge from the dressing room.

Shirts hang in the laundry room, ready to be folded away by Bob 'Oz' Orsborn.

The YTS boys arrive early to clean the players' boots before training. Each boy has responsibility for particular players' boots.

He made it his New Year's resolution to give up smoking but he was back on the cigarettes within the first few days. 'The Man United game didn't help,' he said. Chelsea lost that third round tie 5–3 and with it their chance of retaining the FA Cup. He tried acupuncture in the spring but that didn't work either. He only went once. He is still smoking his roll-ups.

Inside the pavilion, Oz is getting ready for the busiest part of his day, the time when the players stream back in after training and strip off their kits. Then the whole process of washing and drying sixty sets of training kit begins. It is football tradition that the kit man is the first to arrive at training and the last to leave and at Chelsea that tradition is scrupulously observed.

Oz at least has a small army of helpers. It is the responsibility of the YTS boys to look after the boots of the thirty-five professionals on Chelsea's books. Shayne Demetrious, seventeen, is one of them. He gets in at 9 a.m. every morning and he has to look after Gullit's boots and Mafe's and Williams's, Gullit, he says, is quite fussy.

In the afternoons, after boots have been scrubbed and dried and then polished and shined, the YTS boys clean out the showers, the dressing rooms and the medical rooms and only then are they free to go.

The buck stops with Oz, though. He has to organise the transportation of boots and kit to away matches and on foreign trips and if things go wrong, there can be tantrums. Oz will not say it, but Sinclair has the worst reputation among the YTS boys for being over-zealous about his boots. He worries if there is even a speck of black polish on one of the studs and wants it removed immediately. 'Let's just say he likes gleaming match boots,' Oz says.

'Some of them wear very old boots. Dennis Wise has old boots, so old that the leather is hard before every game and he has to smash them with a hammer to soften them up. There might be rips on them so he will get the rip stitched up and then the rip will go again and he will get it stitched up again. Dan Petrescu says the Romanians like wearing new boots every game so he goes through loads.

'In theory, the boots should look after themselves with the YTS boys doing it but I have to paper over the cracks. Some players are not worried, some are very meticulous. With Frank, I think it's the way he expresses a bit of his nervousness before the game. Someone like Mark Hughes, he might not wear tatty boots, but if something happened like I forgot his boots, he wouldn't make a song and dance about it, he would just wear another boot. Somebody else might have a little tantrum.

'I have been here three years and I know the players are appreciative of all the work I do even if they call me lazy. It can be stressful especially if you go to a game and forget something, which thankfully hasn't happened to me so far this season. Boots would be the biggest problem, or a shirt. Ruud was very quiet before a game and he looks how players are and he would be upset with me if I caused an unnecessary worry in a player.' The YTS boys shoulder some of the burden for laying out the kit, too. Oz washes and dries it but a group of the youth-team players arrives at 8.30 a.m. each morning to lay it out in the players' places ready for them when they get in. There are fewer idiosyncrasies in this area although Vialli is the only one who gives his underwear to the kit man so that he can wash that, too, and lay it out for him.

If the kit man's job has its tensions, though, they are multiplied for the physios. Injury is a debilitating, depressing part of everyday life at a football club and fast, smooth, efficient recovery is one of the most

The injured Gustavo Poyet discusses his rehabilitation with first-team coach Graham Rix.

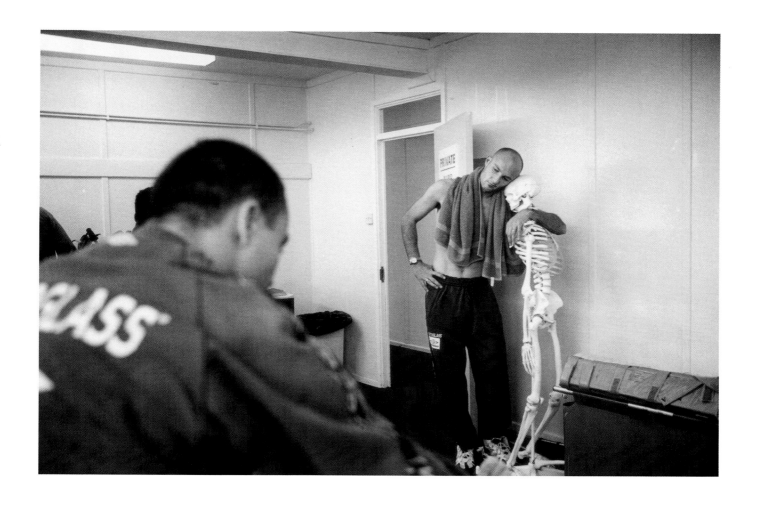

Frank Leboeuf gets up close and personal with a skeleton in the physio's room.

crucial aspects of the progress of any club, especially if the injuries befall key players.

Early in the season, during training, the club's Uruguayan midfield player, Gustavo Poyet, ruptured the cruciate ligaments in a knee, one of the most serious injuries that can happen to a footballer. He was out for the rest of the year. Graeme Le Saux missed five weeks with a dislocated elbow. Celestine Babayaro broke a bone in a foot twice, Eddie Newton had the same injury. One morning at the beginning of the year, Babayaro, a Nigerian international who was the very image of athleticism and grace under pressure before he arrived at Chelsea from Anderlecht the previous summer, emerged gingerly from the physio's room, the foot encased in plaster and cushioned by a huge flip-flop to keep it dry.

It was almost deserted in the pavilion as the shouts of the players drifted in from the training field and Babayaro hobbled tentatively and agonisingly slowly from one end of the corridor to the other on his crutches, backwards and forwards, backwards and forwards, as though enduring some form of torture. It was the second time he had sustained the injury. Like Duberry, he could see his chances of a place in his country's squad for the World Cup receding with every painful step. 'You've not had much luck since you've been here,' someone said to him. He just smiled weakly.

They are a strange phenomenon at any club, injured players. There is sympathy for them but there seems to be a degree of ruthlessness in their treatment. They seem to be largely ignored by the rest of the players, banished to the periphery, almost subconsciously, as if the rest do not want to acknowledge their own vulnerability.

It can take a long time for them to make it back, too. Fitness lost during inactivity is fitness that has to be regained and while the others do much of their work with a ball, those who are recovering have to start with running. 'It's never really a case of having to hold them back,' Mafe says. 'They don't want to do it. They don't like running.'

Mike Banks, the chief physio, does all the clinical assessment of initial injuries and has total control of all things medical. If a player comes in with a cough, a cold, flu or a virus, he deals with it. If they need an appointment at a dentist, he makes it. But when the recovery starts, some of the recuperating players are put in the care of his assistant, Terry Byrne.

Terry is a popular figure at Harlington, a genuine bloke who is just the right mix of earnest and jocular that a physio needs to be to put his patients at ease. He supervised Newton's recovery from a broken leg the season before last and last season he was entrusted with Poyet. 'He's one of mine,' he says.

In the early stages, when the Uruguayan's knee could not take any weight, he and Terry would drive round the corner from the training ground to the pool at the Holiday Inn. Poyet started his recovery by doing simulated running exercises in the deep end for six weeks with Terry beside him. After that, he progressed to exercises in the gym and walking round the pitches in the afternoon, first for twenty minutes then for three-quarters of an hour, gradually picking up the pace.

Terry's reward, his job satisfaction, came fifty-eight minutes into Chelsea's game with Tottenham Hotspur at Stamford Bridge on 11 April when Poyet strode back on to the field to tumultuous applause to resume his career. Five days after that, the Uruguayan scored one of the goals that swept the club past Vicenza into the Cup Winners' Cup final.

'I knew he was going to score against Vicenza,' Terry says. 'I don't know why. I said it before the

Gwyn Williams chats to Dennis Wise as Wise is given treatment on an injured toe by assistant physio Terry Byrne.

The moment of truth: the squad list for a Cup Winners' Cup tie goes up on the board. A black line through a name means exclusion.

Fan mail for the players.

game. With any long-term rehabilitation you rely on the player's own self-motivation. You tell them what to do, give them their instructions. But it is up to them essentially. You have to be a hard bastard with some of them. But Gustavo was one of them that I had to pull the reins back because he was so positive in everything he did. His recovery is down to his own self-motivation.

'I wasn't worried about any of the tackles he went in for in those early games because I have smashed him myself. First of all, you build up the strength with the muscles around the knee, then there is his aerobic work. The last stage of his progression is that he has got to have a 50-50 between me and him because I cannot throw him back into training if he has got any doubt in his own mind.

'But still that is not the same as a geezer coming in on a 50-50 with him in a match. I watched him in his first game back in the reserves and he was putting himself about as usual. The first time he had a really shuddering challenge, it was with Andy Myers in training. I was watching on the touchline and the heart was in the mouth a bit but they both just got up laughing. At first you have a slight worry in the back of your mind but it soon disappears.

'The best part of my job is the mental side, working one on one with the players. It is my job to pick them up. There are days when they are pissed off, when the first team is doing well perhaps and they have to watch them out training while they are stuck inside doing weights but we have been lucky with the players we have had here: their attitude has been spot on. It has great bonuses for us, too. I worked with Eddie Newton for nearly a year from the day he broke his leg and then he came back and scored the second goal in the Cup Final win in 1997. That was all the reward I needed.'

THE END OF EVERY MORNING TRAINING SESSION brings its own rituals. Most of the players wander straight back to the changing rooms and head for the showers. If it is the day before a game, they stop to look at the notice board and the vertical line of names on the squad list. If they are not included in the eighteen or so players Vialli or Gullit has picked to travel to the match, their name is scored through in black, so that it is hard to read what it actually spelt in the first place.

Most stand there expressing no emotion whether they are in or out. Most know but there are a few on the edges of the first team who approach it with trepidation. Youngsters such as Nick Crittenden or players coming back from injury such as Dmitri Kharine, who waits for the confirmation of his return, wait to see their names unobscured by that funereal black line. Sometimes, there are other things on the board, a rota for players' appearances at the Chelsea Megastore, a list of lap times recorded by the players at a night out they had at a kart track in north London (Jody Morris was fastest, Vialli second, Leboeuf third and Di Matteo last). Once, somebody had pinned up a picture of a streaker performing at a Chelsea game: another time, there was a Pooh guide up there which had nothing to do with the bear of the same name. Underneath the board, there are about forty letter-boxes for players and staff where fan mail is sent down from the Bridge to be collected.

The last player off the pitch, almost without fail, is Gianfranco Zola. He never has to look to see whether his name is on the squad list but he is one of the hardest workers in the team. Every day after training, he stays out on the pitch for an extra half hour, striving and striving to perfect the devastating free-kicks that have caused so much damage in the Premiership.

Gary drags a wall of lifesize plastic cut-out men out of the pavilion and across to the pitch nearest the road and the cab drivers and fans, who have parked their cars on the grass verge to gaze idly at the routine training, put down their papers and give their full attention to Zola and the unfortunate goalkeeper he has brought with him to be his patsy.

Sometimes, a couple of spellbound YTS boys are sitting on the grass nearby, watching as the Italian forward takes kick after kick, swinging his right foot at thin air again and again at first to practise the action of wrapping his right foot round the right side of the ball. A long line of balls is grouped in a row about twenty yards out and Zola goes to work. His accuracy is wonderful to behold. Perhaps two out of every three kicks leave the goalkeeper flat-footed as they fly into different corners of the net, right and left, high and low. It must be one of the most dispiriting jobs in football being Zola's fall guy on those mornings, picking ball after ball out of the net, realising that someone has come close to perfecting the art of beating goalkeepers in these situations. Eventually, he drags himself away, ambles back to the pavilion and signs a few autographs. Behind him, the boys try to imitate him. They soon give up. There are others who are always late up for lunch, too. Some go to the gym to lift weights. Mark Hughes is particularly keen on building up his upper body strength. Others like a long, soothing massage. Either Di Matteo or Petrescu usually is the last into the canteen. 'Petrescu always keeps us waiting,' Sian says. 'He says it's because he's a legend.'

There is a casual, informal atmosphere up there. Chatter and laughter echo through the long room that is more like a gallery as more and more players sit down at the trestle tables. Most of them don't bother queuing up at the food bar. They just wander into the kitchen, have a chat with the girls, serve up their food and wander out to sit down. There is not a vegetarian among them.

A few days before Christmas, they always have a party here. The YTS boys sing for the boot money that the senior players give them and the staff, men such as Rix and Williams, dress up in dinner jackets and bow ties to serve the players their lunches. The highlight, though, is when the new players have to sing. Last Christmas, it was Le Saux, Granville, De Goey, Lambourde and Babayaro. De Goey was the only memorable one. He sang some sort of Dutch folk song and then he let the professionals take over. Frode Grodas gave himself the brightest moment of a miserable year by leaping on to a table and belting out a Norwegian folk song so energetically that he fell from his perch. One of the YTS boys, Stephen Broad, who had wowed the audience with a Madonna number the year before, dressed up in drag again and sang 'It's Raining Men'.

For the rest of the year, things are a little bit quieter. Under Hoddle, the rules on diet were much stricter. Gullit relaxed them. He said that if the players wanted to gorge themselves on fast food, they would do it away from his gaze. He will know because it will be reflected in their performance on the pitch but why try to restrict them too heavily while they are at training?

Instead, he placed the emphasis on simple, unfussy dishes. He detested sauces with foods, hated barbecue sauce in particular. Sian does a daily shop at Tesco in Bracknell that usually comes to about £130 for breakfast and lunch. Lunch is usually a variation on a theme of rice or pasta. It is high carbohydrate, low-fat, low-sugar stuff. The odd lasagne, a curry here and there, they all have their day. Zola has a predilection for toasted cheese and ham sandwiches, Kharine likes salad, Vialli insists on sniffing everything to see if it is fresh.

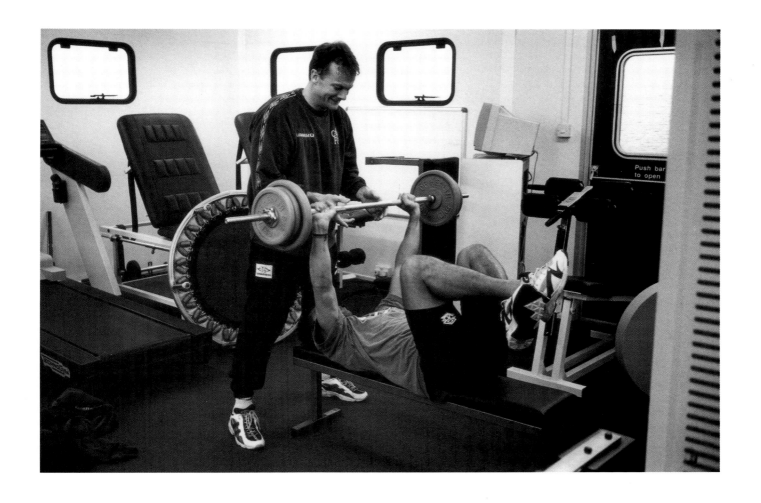

Frode Grodas helps Di Matteo in the weight room.

Christmas in the canteen: Frode Grodas does his party piece.

IT WAS A GREY MONDAY SOON AFTER New Year when I went to my first Chelsea reserve match. You do not feel as if you are setting off for a football match when you herd yourself on to the commuter train at Waterloo with all the men and women in suits grinding their way back to the suburbs after a day labouring in the metropolis. By the time you get off at New Malden, a few stops down the line, having stood all the way, of course, you feel as exhausted and dispirited as they look.

The walk at the other end doesn't help much, either. The High Street in New Malden has not much to recommend it in the cold and the rain. Kingston Road isn't much better either, with its non-descript modern houses and flats and the occasional twenty-four-hour garage. It is probably about half an hour's walk from the station before you start to see the dim glow of the floodlights.

This is Kingsmeadow, the home of Kingstonian, the place where Chelsea play all their home reserve games. Every team has an alter ego like this. Manchester United play their reserve matches at Gigg Lane, the home of Bury FC. The United players call it Pig Lane because the pitch is in such a dreadful state. West Ham's reserves play at Roots Hall, the home of Southend. Everyone has a cross to bear.

From the outside, Kingsmeadow looks like a Sainsbury's or a Safeway. It is on its own small plot, set back from Kingston Road with a reasonably-sized car park and a new redbrick frontage. There is a bar in the centre looking out on to the car park. If it didn't look like a superstore, the next guess would be a leisure centre, not a football stadium.

Inside, it feels even more like a leisure centre. There are a few Chelsea fans in the bar but they are drinking with the air of regulars in their local, playing pool and chewing the fat. Children run around excitedly. Old men in flat caps sit on the long uphol-stered benches that run down one side of the room. Outside, in the foyer, there are some teenage girls in shell suits giggling and darting outside occasionally to whisper secrets in each other's ears before running back inside again.

At the back of the foyer, Jack, the old boy with the black-rimmed glasses and the long beige mack who guards the press entrances to all Chelsea games as ferociously as Cerberus guarded the entrance to Hades, sat behind a desk that was covered with small brown paper envelopes. They were the comps, the complimentary tickets doled out to the scouts who hover over reserve-team matches like hawks.

I never asked Jack why he did the job, what his history was, whether he had once played for Chelsea, whether he just had nothing better to do, or whether he was the ticket man because it gave him a power surge. I suspect it was because he had some sort of lasting affection for the club and that it kept him from being alone but I was always too busy locked in some sort of futile shouting match with him about missing accreditation to find out. I doubt he would have told me anyway.

Once Jack has been negotiated, though, watching Chelsea reserves becomes an altogether more pleasant experience. The best thing about it is that it is like going back to an age when football was more immediate, more accessible to the fans. They are real football people, the people who go to these games, some of them disenfranchised by the prices they have to pay at Stamford Bridge, some of them who just want to get closer to the action than they ever could in the Premiership, to feel the heart of the game beating again.

In many ways, it is a little like going to watch a lower-division game, a bit like the old days. I remember going to watch Stockport County in the early

Eighties when they were still bottom of the old Fourth Division and the whiff of cigar smoke puffed out by men in camelhair coats filled the nostrils.

To watch the reserves is to recapture the essence of the game, to revel in its honesty and its purity of effort. It is to see the striving of the hopefuls, the promise of the future and the autumn of the ones whose time in the first team has been and gone. You can grasp the soul of football here more than ever you can in the midst of 35,000 on a Saturday afternoon. Half an hour before the kick-off, there are only ever a handful of spectators in the stadium. There is no need to come any earlier. There is only one stand. There are always seats available. Many stand on the terraces that cover the other three sides of the stadium anyway, just for old time's sake.

When the players jog out for their warm-up, there is no cheer from the crowd because there is no crowd. The area around the players' tunnel, though, is an autograph hunter's heaven and ten or fifteen teenagers are gathered there to try to grab signatures from Frank Sinclair, making his way back from injury, and David Rocastle, before he finally got his move away from Chelsea to Malaysia. Players on the fringe of the first team, such as Paul Hughes and Mark Nicholls, are also popular targets.

They all sign happily as they come out of the tunnel. More than that, they stand and chat. A couple of spivs slid down from the stands to talk to Sinclair. They looked like agents, old-style agents, late middle-aged, overcoats, rasping voices and gritty laughs. And, of course, broad Cockney accents. Sinclair looked as though he was humouring them but they chatted and smiled for a few minutes and then he turned on his heels to join his teammates on the far side of the pitch.

By now, a grey-haired man in suit trousers and a striped shirt that is struggling to restrain his bulging

gut has wandered out on to the touchline to talk to the groundsman. Inside, he serves drinks at the bar. Quarter of an hour before kick-off, some of the YTS boys, who act as ballboys for the reserves, come running back in, clutching take-away pizza boxes.

Inside, in the home changing room at the foot of the stand, Mick McGiven, the reserve-team coach, is preparing his team talk for that night's match against Southampton. In a side-room, Mark Stein, once a highly-prized first-team regular, now an outsider, is having a massage, lying flat on his stomach. A strong smell of Deep Heat emanates from his direction.

The main body of the changing room is square, modern and functional. A couple of the team are playing head tennis in the middle of it with a kit bin for a net. A sheet of paper has been pinned up on a notice board by the door which says, simply, WALLS. Instructions have been written on it, saying that Mark Nicholls, playing just two days after he scored two goals for the first team against Coventry City, Rocastle, Paul Hughes and Stein, are the players designated to be in the defensive wall if Southampton win any free-kicks on the edge of the Chelsea area. Jody Morris is the one picked out to be on the end of the wall, trying to charge the shot down.

Rocastle, twice a league championship winner with Arsenal and a player who has been transferred twice for £2 million, had fallen on hard times by the stage of his career when he reached Chelsea and he could find no place in the team either under Gullit or Vialli, but in his time as captain of the reserves he was a model professional.

At Kingsmeadow, just as at Harlington, he was the hub of the team. In the build-up to the match, he was a fount of advice to the young players who respected him for what he had achieved in the past and the whole-hearted attitude he continued to exhibit even now when no longer in the limelight.

David Rocastle studies a diagram of tactics for a reserve game.

Reserve-team coach Mick McGivern gives advice to young hopeful Paul Hughes in the Kingstonian dressing room.

He tells the left-back that even if he gets half a yard of space when he is attacking then he must try to whip a cross in. He keeps saying 'End product' all the time, trying to instil into the players that they have to make every pass and run count. Then he goes methodically round the room, shaking everybody's hand in a pre-match ritual. 'We've got ninety minutes to win the game,' he tells everyone. 'We do not have to win the game in the first ten minutes.'

Rumours about the reasons for Rocastle's fall from grace have circulated in football ever since he failed to make it at Leeds United, maybe even since George Graham bombed him out of Highbury. They have got more and more extreme with every year that he has spent in the wilderness, from unfounded whispers about drugs to speculation about the state of his knees to shrugs that he had not got the hunger any more.

One night at Kingsmeadow disproves all of them at a stroke. 'I have been desperate for first-team football,' Rocastle said. 'I know people have been saying I am just picking up my wage packet and that I have priced myself out of the market with other teams but it is not like that. I would go to Hartlepool if I had to to restart my career.

'Sometimes, it is hard playing in the reserves. Without a doubt. Especially when you have had a taste of what the other side of the game is like. But I have always done my best. I have always tried to help the younger lads and set them an example and try to pass on some of my experience and I hope they respect me for it. I gave it all I had here but it doesn't seem to have worked out for me.'

Before they go out on to the pitch, McGiven has the last word. Once the manager at Ipswich Town, he is another widely respected figure in football and has helped to bring the crop of young players who are on the fringes of the Chelsea first team through to the position they are in. He urges the team to be positive right from the kick-off.

There is the sound of studs banging harshly on the floor as they do their final warm-up. McGiven tells them to look at the board for their markings at corners. George Price, the assistant physio, starts throwing used tops into the kit bin. The room is a hive of activity now, not stillness. The players walk around nervously, wander into another section to go to the toilet. Some sit and secure their socks with their tie-ups as McGiven gives them their instructions. Nick Crittenden and Paul Hughes juggle with a ball in the middle of the floor.

They all want to win. Which footballer does not? But the priority in the reserves is to impress. Chelsea and McGiven do not care about winning the Football Combination, the league for the reserves. They finished in the lower half of the table. Arsenal were top. The priority is to bring the younger players further along the path towards the first team. For the older ones, whose chance has gone, there is always the possibility that one of the watching scouts, will recommend that another club resurrects their career.

In the 98/99 season, for instance, Leon Knight, the prodigy who has been studying at the FA School of Excellence at Lilleshall, may make more appearances. He has already played for England Schoolboys and the commercial interest in him from kit manufacturers and sponsors has alarmed Chelsea, who feel that their prospect may be ruined. Independent observers rate Knight and Joe Cole, who is on West Ham's books, as the two best schoolboy prospects in the country.

'Some of the other clubs treat their reserves as a sop to the players who can't get in the first team,' McGiven says, 'but we have never done that at Chelsea, not recently anyway. Our policy is to give youth a chance and to play as many of them as we

Before the match: Nick Crittenden gets in some juggling practice while other reserves prepare with stretching exercises.

can. Obviously we balance it up with a few experienced pros but it is a different discipline to league football because we are not going out to win the league. We are trying to develop players and that is something that is a lot harder to quantify.'

Against Southampton, Nicholls was called up at the last minute because Laurent Charvet, the Frenchman who was later to sign professional terms, had not then got clearance to begin his trial. Even though he had just played for the first team, Nicholls, a promising young striker, was happy to turn out.

'It's not hard to get motivated for games like this after the first team,' Nicholls said. 'I was happy to play. It is no different to playing in front of 30,000. Your job is your job. You just play to the best of your ability. There are a lot of young lads trying to impress and a lot on the fringe of the first team and you have got the assistant manager here looking at you. The boys have got a lot to prove to everyone.'

There is a warning pinned up on one of the dressing room doors saying 'Please stay out of the goalmouths until fifteen minutes before kick-off.' Everyone has heeded it. Finally, just as they are preparing to go out, the warning bell that is the signal for every Premiership and Nationwide League player to leave the dressing room to make for the pitch rings out shrilly. They line up behind Rocastle, jogging up and down on the spot, shouting at each other in encouragement, and then they stride out.

The pitch is rough and uneven with great swathes of brown in the centre circle and the goalmouths. The glare from the floodlights seems ten times less bright than at Premiership games, like a symbol of the gloom that has enveloped the careers of some of the players on view. They bathe the ground in a sort of eerie glow and make the half-hearted chants and shouts that come from the crowd sound hollow.

At Kingsmeadow, there is just one tiny redbrick stand along one touchline. Its seats go about six rows deep. The other three sides are shallow terracing ringed by corrugated iron or walls of concrete blocks. The advertising hoardings are few and far between but there is one for the Hotel Antoinette behind the goal and another for Cherry Red Records alongside it.

Chelsea do not play their usual combination of players against Southampton. A lot of the young apprentices are involved in an FA Youth Cup match at Tranmere two days later so they are unavailable. Sinclair plays but does not stand out. Nicholls has his collar up and a slightly haughty air. Stein looks sharp and dangerous in attack. Rocastle gives it his all. Occasionally, McGiven's head pops up above the dugout to bawl out instructions.

From time to time, another of those commuter trains from Waterloo rumbles past in the night with its cargo of drained souls, its lights flickering in the distance, a reminder to the young men who are trying to pursue their dream out on the pitch of the humdrum life that might be lying in wait for them if they do not make it, if they fail on cold Monday nights like this.

Even the referees have a lot at stake in these matches. They are on probation, too. They are linesmen in the Nationwide League and these are their big chances to impress an assessor and get themselves at the head of the list to be upgraded for the next season. Hence, there are plenty of bookings. Neil Clement, Chelsea's central defender, becomes the biggest victim when he is sent off for an innocuous tackle.

In the central section of the main stand, Gwyn Williams is sitting with Graham Rix and Eddie Niedzwiecki, watching keenly. Williams, like many of the other stalwarts at Harlington, is Chelsea through and through, a man who has defied the fickleness of football by surviving a host of managers and recording eighteen years unbroken service in the backroom staff. He has seen the genesis of the modern club, he knows its grass roots better than anyone, and he is convinced that the much-maligned Bates deserves much of the credit.

His title now is assistant manager, although he is referred to variously as general manager, public relations manager and administration manager. He is all things to all men at Chelsea, the man who knows the place and its mores best, who has seen it evolve into the power it is today, and who stands at its nerve centre.

'I have been here eighteen years now,' he says. 'I had played semi-pro football with Kingstonian, Wembley, Hayes, St Albans, Maidenhead, Ruislip, Wimbledon, Slough Town. If it was a team in London, I'd played for it.

'Then I became a PE and Maths teacher. I was deputy in charge of pastoral. I looked after all the bad boys. They took more and more of the good things off me. They wanted me sorting out the glue-sniffers and the smokers. Then, when Geoff Hurst was appointed manager at Chelsea, he sacked everybody and advertised the jobs in the *Daily Telegraph*. I applied for every job and got the one at the bottom, youth development officer. My brief was to get the best young kids in and through the years we have had a fair few in.

'Then, I moved on to youth-team coach, reserve-team coach, first-team coach under Bobby Campbell, chief scout, then I came up and sideways and down. Then, when Glenn Hoddle came, I was chief scout and now I am really general manager. I do all the admin, all the organising for when we go away, I have done all that. Hotels, travel, food, what time the bus leaves.

'I deal with the day-to-day inquiries about buying players and selling players. If someone wants to sell a player, they come to me. If we want to sell a player, I liaise with Colin Hutchinson and if we can agree a price, we sell him. It is a triangle, really: Luca, Colin and myself. The finance is agreed by Colin but when the new players come in, it is down to me. I look after their accommodation, hotels, all that.

'When I first came here, I was bright and young. Then, in my first couple of weeks here I was told "don't bring any kids in, there's no money". There was me, having given up a good job teaching being told there was no money to bring triallists in. That was on the Friday. On the Saturday, we had the opening game of the season against Wrexham in the league and I bumped into the chairman on the way in and he said "Oh Gwyn, do us a favour, take all that crate of champagne upstairs for the directors".

'I was disillusioned. I thought "What have I done?". But it has changed massively and the revolution has been from the top. The place was dying on its feet until Ken Bates came in. We have had the leadership from the top. He has been a one-man crusade. I have got nothing but admiration for what he has achieved. And the last three managers here have been a revolution.'

When the half-time whistle blows, Williams, Rix and the rest leap up off their seats and head for what might pass as the executive bar downstairs. This, too, is like a scene from football's past, a place where real football men, unreconstructed and unpolluted by football fashions, meet to talk. For fifteen minutes, it becomes a working man's club for football people down there.

A Lolita of a girl in tight black trousers brings cups of tea round to the clusters of middle-aged men and scouts who huddle round in circles, discussing what they have just seen like farmers at a cattle market. Smoke rings waft towards the ceiling, foamy pints of bitter are lined up on the bar, and those who

Far from the stands at Stamford Bridge, Mark Nicholls watches the Southampton keeper snuff out the attack during a reserves match at Kingstonian.

Graham Rix enjoys a half-time cup of tea with safety officer Keith Lacey and friends in the homely atmosphere of the Kingstonian bar. Rix keeps a close eye on the progress of the reserves.

have not got their order in earlier queue up in a long line for the tray of sandwiches.

There are scouts down there from nineteen clubs. Brentford, Rotherham, Bolton Wanderers, Plymouth Argyle, Crystal Palace, Fulham, Lincoln City, Huddersfield, Swindon, Wimbledon and Oxford always come. Allan Harris from Reading and Andy King from Sunderland are there. They lose themselves in their chatter for quarter of an hour, nodding at old friends and acquaintances, remembering the halcyon days. It is almost like a scene from a Prohibition movie, like a speak-easy hidden from the world where simple pleasures can still be enjoyed. Eventually, they all head back up to the stand.

In the second half, you can sense the vitality of the game even more. You can hear the shouts of the players, hear Sinclair yelling 'Frank's up' as he goes for a header. And behind the goal, the small boys still have the freedom to run around on the terraces, trying to retrieve the ball when it goes high or wide, indulging in the sort of fripperies that are no longer possible in the stadiums of the late ninetiess.

For what it is worth, Chelsea win comfortably. Stein gets two poacher's goals. Southampton, who have a £1m player, Stig Johansen, in their line-up, do not manage any in return. Two minutes from the end, even though he has had hardly anything to do, Dmitri Kharine, who alternates in nets for the reserves with Kevin Hitchcock, shows he is still concentrating hard when he saves well from a Johansen header. Rocastle, who has been an inspiration, throws himself into one shuddering double-footed tackle right on the final whistle that, once

more, makes a mockery of any suggestion he is not committed to the cause.

Afterwards, there is a sense of achievement in the dressing room as the players pad in and out to the shower. The floor is strewn with sweat-stained kit. The YTS boys scurry round, picking it up and throwing it into the bins. Rocastle sits drained on his bench, staring at the floor until he drags himself into the showers.

When they leave, there is no coach to take them to a hotel, no post-match meal or celebration. They all make their own way home. Sometimes, players who have been cosseted in the youth teams of Premiership clubs are sent to the lower divisions to get a taste of reality. Rio Ferdinand, for instance, got his at Bournemouth. He saw the lonely world of digs and washing your own kit and realised how much to be sought after a top-flight professional's life was. At Chelsea the reserves have something of the same purpose, although by lower-division standards they are still relatively spoilt.

Rocastle sits in the bar for half an hour with Stein and some friends. No one comes to ask for his autograph now. He does not seem to expect it. It was as if the supporters who had grabbed him before the game did not know who he was, just that he was wearing a blue shirt. Now he is in civilian clothes, he has returned to his unwelcome anonymity.

They leave with Paul Hughes. Hughes goes to his car and the same gaggle of schoolgirls that haunted the foyer before the game coo around him now. He smiles at them and roars away, screeching his brakes, showing off. In reserve-team football, it's about the only chance you get.

The Match

THIS IS AN ANECDOTE THAT READS a little like a parable, but it is worth telling anyway. It takes place in the Chelsea dressing room, a room that is a close call between a rectangle and a square. Various alcoves spin off it into the corners. At one point, there is a gym, at another there are showers, at another toilets, at another the massage table. And then there are the players. They wander into the room after their pre-match meal about two hours before kick-off. There is a little bit of laughing and joking but mostly they are sombre and quiet. It is here more than anywhere, more even than on those interminable days down at Harlington, that you get an impression of men going about their work, and high-pressure work at that.

Some of them have blank looks on their faces, looks of pure concentration that say they do not want to be bothered, do not even want to be looked at. Others affect levity but it is obvious that they are twisted inside. Some footballers – Gary Megson when he was at Manchester City is an example – get so nervous before games that they vomit. There are none of those at Chelsea but there are some who look as though they might get close.

Anyway, into this picture of tension and barely concealed nerves, comes Dennis Wise like a jack in a box, oblivious to it all. Surprise, surprise, he is the joker in the pack, the one who is hyper-active behind those closed doors, the one who laughs and jokes and swears and generally has scant regard for the sensitivities of those around him. Until he appears, the dressing room is a quietish, thoughtful place.

Early in the season, Wise excelled himself by playing a joke on Zola that could have been straight out of his days with the Crazy Gang at Wimbledon. Zola is one of the many who likes to be still in the hours before the game, who likes to be contemplative. His chosen mode of relaxation is to read spy novels.

Gradually, the players began to notice that the Italian, whose English is getting better and better but who is still a hesitant reader, had been reading the same Raymond Chandler novel for about the first seven home games. He was making progress but it was painfully slow. For a while, it became a bit of a standing joke between the rest of them.

Then, before a mid-season match, Zola put the book down briefly and went out into the tunnel to try to find some friends. Wise seized his chance. He grabbed the book and tore out the last chapter. Then, he put it back exactly where he had found it and when Zola came back, he picked it up not knowing that anything was amiss. Thereafter, there were bouts of suppressed giggles every time Zola opened the book. He just looked at them with a puzzled expression. Eventually, he discovered the joke before the match against Crystal Palace in March in the midst of a long goalless spell and vented his anger on Wise. He promptly scored against Palace and as he was celebrating, Wise ran alongside him and promised he would give him the missing pages back as a reward.

IN ENGLISH FOOTBALL, DRESSING ROOMS ARE still considered sacrosanct. Now and again, perhaps, as at Sunderland, Peterborough United and Leyton Orient, they allow the television cameras in for one of those fly-on-the-wall documentaries and there is a quick and pathetic burst of moral outrage about how much either Peter Reid or Barry Fry swears during the average half-time tirade.

That is usually it. It is like an inner sanctum here,

Zola finds a quiet spot in the gym to focus before the match.

BBC commentator John Motson doing his pre-match preparation in the Stamford Bridge press room.

a place of mystery and wonder and utter privacy. It is hard enough getting players out of it after the game to talk to the media. It is absolutely unheard of for the media to be allowed admittance to the dressing room. That would be considered a violation of players' rights, something that would never, ever be countenanced while the current climate of mutual suspicion between players and press exists.

It is wonderfully different in America, of course. The locker rooms of the National Football League (NFL) teams are open to the media after every training session and before and after matches. The players wander in and out to the showers in a state of undress and routinely conduct their interviews by their lockers as they are getting changed. It is normal for them.

Basketball is even more open. I went to a Chicago Bulls game against Milwaukee Bucks in Milwaukee late last year and wandered into the Bulls locker room, as you are permitted to do, about an hour before the start of the game. Dennis Rodman, he of the tattoos and multi-coloured hair, was sitting in one corner with his earphones on, Pearl Jam blasting into his head. He did not want to talk.

But in another corner, Michael Jordan was sitting on a treatment table, his back propped up against a wall, talking casually to a group of people. I assumed at first they must be friends of his but gradually I realised they were journalists so I sauntered over a little self-consciously to join them and listened in wonder to their conversation.

This was an hour before the game and here was Jordan, probably the greatest athlete in the world, certainly the best paid and the one who most bestrides his sport, sitting there and talking discursively about matters as far removed as his opinions of Shaquille O'Neal and his general philosophy on life. It was fascinating, engrossing stuff. Eventually,

half an hour before the game was due to begin, they kicked us out.

At Stamford Bridge and in English football in general, that sort of situation is probably a generation away. Suspicion has built up over the past two decades, mainly through the activities, not of sports journalists, but of news reporters detailed to cover the private lives of increasingly high-profile players. That many players choose to accept money to write ghosted articles from the perpetrators of these practices only muddies the waters even more.

At Chelsea, journalists pick up their match tickets at the players' entrance half-way along the East Stand. Frank Steer usually shepherds us up the stairs where the ticket is doled out and we are led down the corridor that leads to the tunnel and then siphoned off into the press room. The tunnel is usually awash with people, mainly television crews, radio and security men and the odd sponsors' guest and friends of the players. Keith Lacey, the stadium safety officer, is often there, too, usually with a look of barely suppressed panic on his face.

The press facilities are not the best in the Premiership. Brian, the press steward, is one of the most popular, most amicable in the league but he hasn't got the materials to work with. Ken Bates is very proud of his ladies' toilet but that is about as far as the amenities go.

In Chelsea's favour, they normally provide excellent access to the players. This is largely due to the efforts of Gwyn Williams, who usually guides players who have been requested by the media through to the press room where they will talk for five or ten minutes. At other leading clubs like Manchester United and Arsenal, the players usually ignore all requests and go straight home after a game.

Williams, with one or two exceptions, has a cordial relationship with the newspaper boys, many of whom he has known for much of his eighteen years with the club. He does not suffer fools gladly and does not tolerate any overstepping of boundaries or invasions of privacy at Harlington. Foreign camera crews who do not know the rules are routinely ejected.

Rix, too, is popular with the press. A smoker and a joker, he was the driving force behind arranging a match at Harlington between the staff and the media. He teased us for weeks about how badly they were going to beat us, about who he had got playing where, about how his defence would be sitting in their deckchairs while they dealt with our feeble efforts in attack.

I saw him play in Kevin Hitchcock's testimonial against Nottingham Forest a few days before we were due to play and began to fear the worst. He still has a marvellous touch and a beautiful left foot. He would have run our game and run us into the ground. Then, the day before the game, he rang up to cry off. Terry Byrne and Mike Banks, the physios, had let him down at the last minute, he said, and he did not have enough players. He never heard the end of it.

In this respect and others, Chelsea are ahead of their time in their dealings with the media. The players, perhaps partly because of the more relaxed, courteous attitude of the foreign imports, are almost always willing to stop and talk and the proximity of the press room to the tunnel makes it easier for journalists to dodge out of the door and snatch a few words with Zola or Di Matteo or Hughes as they prepare to fight their way through the crowds of supporters and autograph-hunters to their cars by the entrance.

Many of the faces in the press room change from week to week but there are some fixtures. Neil Barnett, the editor of the *Chelsea Matchday Magazine*

and the man who doubles as the chief writer for *Onside* magazine and as the pitch announcer before games and at half-time, is always there. Hardly a day goes by at Harlington either, without his face appearing around a corner.

Brian Glanville, the veteran reporter of *The Times*, is usually there, too. Glanville, who still puts in the occasional appearance for the local Chelsea Casuals, is one of the most respected football writers in Fleet Street, not just because of his pedigree and experience but because of his glorious irreverence and his refusal to be sycophantic to any of the managers who cross his path. His delight in all things Italian leads him to Chelsea ever more regularly.

Before each game, the press room is a hive of chatter and gossip. Glanville holds forth here, another group whisper in a corner, exchanging information there. Some watch the highlights of previous Chelsea games that are beamed out from the television set up high in a corner, others sift through Bates's programme notes, which are often good for a story, or scan what Gullit or Vialli has to say. The season's statistics, goals, appearances, scores and the rest, always inside the back page, are invaluable.

After a Saturday game, the Sunday newspaper journalists usually stay upstairs in the cramped press box, battering away frantically at their computers to hit their early deadlines. Often, they have to have their report finished by the time the final whistle blows. Then, they get a chance to re-write it for later editions, adding quotes.

Vialli usually takes a considerable time to appear for the post-match press conference, particularly if he has been playing. He always looks dapper, dressed in suit and tie. He sits behind a table and answers questions from the Sunday papers and the phalanx of Italian journalists who are almost permanently attached to Chelsea games because of him, Zola and Di Matteo.

After he has finished his Sunday press conference, Vialli then retreats either to a corner or to a quiet part of the tunnel outside to talk to the Monday papers so that they have a chance to work on a different line from the Sundays. This is where the best and most persistent questioners show themselves, men such as Brian Woolnough of the *Sun*, Lee Clayton of the *Daily Star*, Nigel Clarke of the *Daily Mail* and Rob Shepherd, Martin Samuel and Paul McCarthy of the *Express*.

This session lasts anything up to twenty minutes and often yields back-page stories for Monday morning. Vialli is a wonderful interviewee, just as Gullit was, and although he is careful not to give anything away in terms of transfer news, the emotive terms in which he speaks rarely fail to provide good material for his questioners.

After that is done, everyone begins to drift away. Brian clears up in the press room and someone takes away the empty trays that brought the half-time sandwiches for the media. By 6.30 pm, most of the players have gone too, having run the gauntlet of the supporters outside, and anyone left in the press box is urged to get going lest they get locked in the stadium.

Stamford Bridge, like any empty football ground in the immediate aftermath of a match, is an almost eerie sight by then. Where once, less than ninety minutes ago, all had been colour and passion and noise and animated faces, now there are just empty seats and a deserted arena. Stadiums like that live to be full not empty but somehow, even though there may only be the odd rubbish collector loading crumpled hot dog cartons into black bin-liners, there is still a magical sort of echo about the place. The excitement lingers.

THE SAME EXCITEMENT IS THERE WHEN THE players arrive. This time, it is a tingle of anticipation, partly the apprehension of the unknown, partly the joy of the fact that anything is possible. No matter how early the players arrive, there is a gaggle of supporters – these days it is more often a swollen crowd – to cheer them off the team coach.

If we still take a 3 pm Saturday kick-off as the norm – even though it is fast being overtaken by a host of other Sky-driven times – the players arrive at Stamford Bridge at 11.45 am. Sometimes, they will have spent the night before at their regular hotel on Cromwell Road, close to Gloucester Road tube station, sometimes they will meet at Harlington first. Usually, though, they arrive in the hotel minibus.

They leap out, do what they can to skirt the supporters, and then after a few preliminaries and pleasantries in the tunnel, perhaps sorting out tickets for friends and relatives, they begin their pre-match routine at midday. At 12.30 pm, they dart upstairs to the stadium's main restaurant for their pre-match meal. Just as at Harlington, this can be a variety of things but the staple is pasta. At 1pm, they come back downstairs, walk down the corridor, past the visitors' dressing room on their left and next to that, the press room, past the players' bar on their right and then go through the next door on the right into the sanctuary of their own dressing room. From then until they venture out on to the pitch to be warmed up by Ade Mafe, they do not leave that room.

Sometimes, when they first walk in, there is a bit of shouting, Mafe yelling something at Wise. 'You've done me,' he was yelling before one game this season, joking about something Wise had written about him in the programme. Mafe, though, is not too averse to publicity. He didn't really care. The dressing room is big and clean and stark, more modern and sparse than the antiquated rooms where

Zola is beseiged by fans as he leaves Stamford Bridge. The Italian is one of the players to have brought real international appeal to Chelsea.

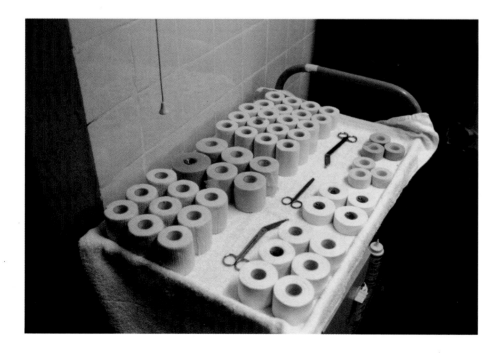

Oz hangs up the kit in the dressing room. Each player likes his kit laid out in a special way.

Rolls of binding for the players' legs.

the players have to prepare at Wembley but not as luxurious as the facilities at Old Trafford which are all wood-panelled and a mass of showers. You might expect it to be uproarious, but apart from Wise and his japes, it is not.

At 1 p.m., Vialli gives a team talk and there are a few adjustments to tactics, and then the players are left to themselves for a while. They are superstitious characters, footballers, and many of them have their own routines that they simply have to follow. Often, the insistence on one particular thing is totally illogical but if it works for them . . .

I had been told that Michael Duberry and Frank Sinclair prefer new socks for each match as opposed to those that have been washed and sure enough, when they walked in, they strode over to their pegs with a sense of urgency to check that that the socks were there, unsullied. It is another example of the ways in which Sinclair tries to rid himself of the tension that builds up.

Some players like more space than others, some ask Oz the kit man to get them more pegs. Most have their own set places. Hughes and Vialli, for instance, have adjoining pegs. Vialli likes a lot of space, and several of them like to spread all their kit and belongings out. If you have an image of a tidy, ordered dressing room, it is inaccurate.

A lot of them do not like having their shirts hung up on the pegs. They prefer it if it is just flopped casually where they sit. That is one of Di Matteo's idiosyncrasies in particular. He goes one step further and puts all his kit on the floor. His part of the bench will be clear and his match shirt and shorts will be on the floor with people walking over it and sometimes slipping on it. Occasionally, Oz will pick it up and put it back on the bench but Di Matteo just puts it down on the floor again.

Then, there is the bewildering variety of kit they have to choose from. This extends far beyond a simple choice of size of shirt and shorts. There are underclothes, short sleeves, long sleeves, tapered necks, polo necks, necks with the collar snipped off with scissors. It goes on and on.

Wise has his own vest which he has had for years. There are sleeveless cotton shirts, there are long-sleeve cotton shirts. There are white thermal thick t-shirts and there is a sleeveless thermal. Vialli wears a sleeveless cotton t-shirt but will cut the seam off it. If he has a long-sleeve cotton t-shirt, he will cut the neck off. He feels uncomfortable when restricted.

Vialli has his own underpants, too. Some have cycling shorts, some like to warm up in track-suit bottoms. Wise, Steve Clarke, Andy Myers, and Mark Hughes will wear short-sleeved shirts no matter how cold it is. Duberry, Eddie Newton and Jody Morris will wear long sleeves all the time even when it is hot.

So when Chelsea play away, Oz sometimes has to take four shirts for every player. 'They have a warm up t-shirt,' Oz says, 'and they will chuck that, towel down and then put on their under t-shirt and then put their shirt on. Supposing I have not got a short-sleeve shirt for one of them, then some of them would cut the sleeves off before the game.

'The shirt that comes for Zola is usually miles too long so I have to get it tailored. Names get stitched on by Umbro. For a three o'clock game, I sometimes go to lay the kit out the previous evening. Usually, I would get down there at say 10 am. They virtually all sit in the same place. A lot of them like bobble hats and gloves when they go out. Some of them insist on the black, they don't really want the blue ones.'

When the complicated issue of the kit has been settled, the players go into what are called their 'preps', their preparations for the game. Once more, this tends to be an intensely individualistic thing, full of strange superstitions and rituals that sometimes date back to lucky matches, but sometimes date back to matches that were a disaster.

All the players have a massaging rub before the game, administered by Terry Byrne or Mike Banks. Ed De Goey likes to go first on these, Duberry, for some reason, always goes third. Because of time constraints, each player is limited to about ten or fifteen minutes attention from the physios.

'Before the match, the rubs that they get act to stimulate blood circulation. While some, like Hughes and Zola read and some listen to music, others, like Dan Petrescu, go into their own stretching routine for about an hour. Some of them play a little game of head tennis, others will get their strappings ready, others, like Wise, become hyper.

Then there are the strappings. 'Each player has different needs,' Byrne says. 'Some may have damaged ankles, some may use it to prevent going over on their ankle, to support their ankles. There is an elastic adhesive tape but there is also a zinc oxide tape which fixes the ankle into position.'

Strapped up, kitted up and rubbed down, most of them wander out on to the pitch about half an hour before the game and Mafe begins his warm-up routine with them. They run for a while back and forth across the pitch in a long line, exercising, turning, sprinting. Then, at the sharp end, as kick-off approaches, they do some sprints against a partner. Finally, they jog back to the dressing room to be given a final team talk, latterly by Rix.

The influence and input of Rix has increased dramatically since the demise of Gullit and accession of Vialli. Finally, he is being given the credit that he has been due for so long and the responsibility on which he thrives but which Gullit never gave him.

Vialli is in charge throughout the week and in training but when the pre-match routine begins, he hands over the reins to his coach and lets him take charge. He gives the team talks, he dishes out the dressing-downs, he decides the substitutions.

The first real test of his authority came at the end of the disappointing Cup Winners' Cup semi-final first leg defeat to Vicenza in Italy. Petrescu, substituted midway through the second half for tactical reasons, had spat on the floor in Rix's direction as he left the pitch and stormed straight down the touch-line to the dressing rooms. Something had to be done after such a show of petulance and Rix did not shirk the task.

'Luca backs me,' Rix said. 'He thinks the same as me. I started speaking after the game and then I remembered the thing with Petrescu. And in front of all the boys I said "By the way Dan, you ever bloody look at me again and spit on the floor and I will come over and punch your face in." His bottle went a little bit and he muttered under his breath.

'But Luca looked at him and said "If you've got something to say, Dan, say it. Say it now, come on. Why do you think you were brought off? You were brought off because you weren't performing. It's not because we don't like you. If you don't perform you don't play." I put my head on the line and I got Luca's backing, so fair play to him. We are exactly on the same wavelength as far as most things are concerned. He is not so egotistical that he thinks he doesn't need help from anybody.

'In the long term, I suppose I would like to be my own man. At the moment, I am more than happy doing what I'm doing. Luca thinks he's learning it but I'm learning it, too. There was a big question mark for me whether I could have the same influence with top-class pros as I had had with the youth team and the reserve team. And I have found in the last two and a half months, that I can. When I speak, people do shut up and listen. Before, I would do all the doggy work but in terms of getting up and speaking, I wouldn't do it because Rudi didn't want me to. Whereas Luca does. Back in April, when Luca didn't play against Sheffield Wednesday, he still wanted me to speak. If there are any bollockings, it is me who does it.'

For the fans, some things in the build-up to the game have changed, some have remained the same. There is more to do at the stadium now in the hours leading up to the kick-off than there once was. Gone are the days when you wandered on to the terraces, sat down on one of the concrete steps and leafed exhaustively through the programme until the players came out to warm up.

Now there is a whole host of entertainments. There are re-runs of Chelsea goals to watch on the televisions in the eating areas. The food has been upgraded even though it is still far from the best in the Premiership, and there are the hostelries of Chelsea Village to take advantage of now. The Shed bar, in particular, is always heaving with fans before matches.

The most popular pre-match haunt, though, is Rosie's, a pub-cum-live music joint on Fulham Road between Fulham Broadway tube station and the main entrance to the stadium. Its sides seem to bulge on match days with the volume of people inside and the decibel level of the music and the chanting.

There are bouncers on the door, but that is more to regulate the flow of customers than to watch for trouble. The only danger, usually, is overcrowding and the landlord, a formidable-looking Irishman called John McCabe, insists he has not had one unseemly incident in the ten years he has been in charge.

There are a whole range of pubs in Fulham Road and its environs, and hotels and restaurants, too. The more affluent sometimes make a day of it and go for a spot of lunch on Kings Road or around Sloane Square and Knightsbridge. Most still pile off the tube and grab a hamburger at one of the stalls or some chips at the Chelsea Kebab House next door to the station.

In the late Seventiess and early Eightiess, the Chelsea fans were notorious for their involvement in hooliganism and crowd violence. But that is part of the old Chelsea that has all but disappeared. Some of this, perhaps, may be due to the changing social profile among the fans, the fact that a lot of the old trouble makers cannot afford the luxury of buying a ticket for a Premiership match any more and are looking elsewhere, but much of it is to do with sensitive and alert policing, too. In this respect, Chelsea are fortunate that the officer in charge is a man whose modern thinking and openness is a refreshing change from the closed hostility that used to dominate many forces' dealings with football fans. Policing Chelsea used to be a nightmare assignment but in past years it has grown steadily easier. And while the players are going through their pre-match routines, binding their battered ankles up with tape and choosing whether they are going to wear short sleeves or long sleeves, the police are in the midst of a pre-match routine of their own.

'I am not completely qualified to judge how much the job of policing Chelsea has changed,' says Superintendent Anthony Wills, Divisional Commander at Fulham Police Station and the man in charge of operations at both Stamford Bridge and Craven Cottage, 'because I have only been here for a year. But I have spoken to people who were here in the past and I know people who have been here over that period.

'The policing of Chelsea has changed and the type of people going has changed slightly. It is probably more because they are getting full attendances

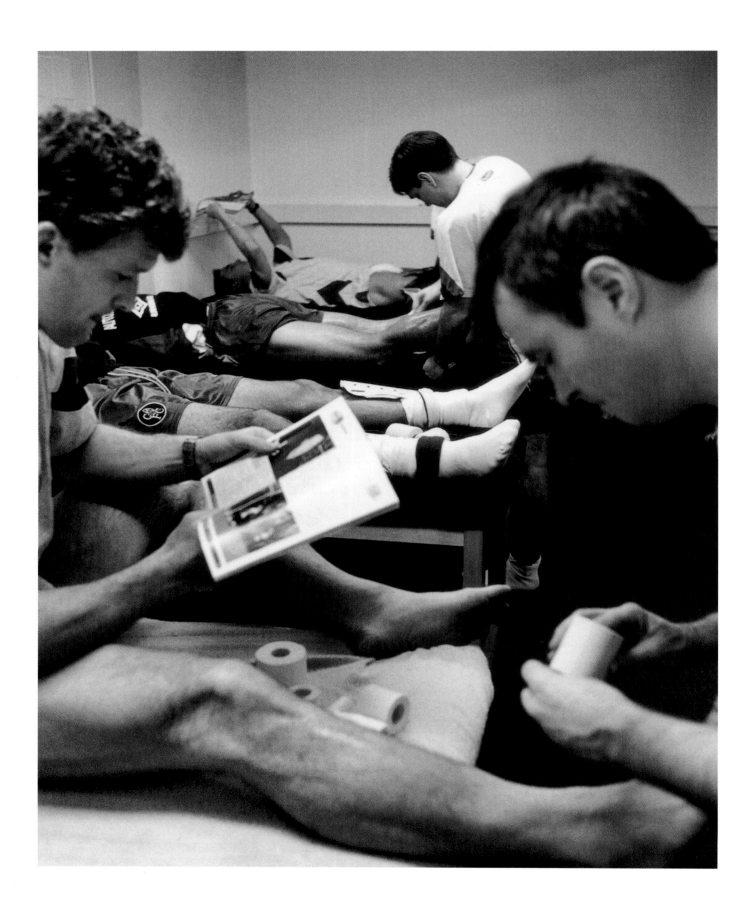

The long wait: the players
spend several hours in the
dressing room before a
match. Mark Hughes reads
a programme as the physio
binds his legs, Roberto
Di Matteo reads the paper,
while Frank Leboeuf sorts
out some tickets for guests.

Before the players
arrive, the assistant
physios play games in
the dressing room.

Street life. On the Fulham Road local residents go about their life as the Chelsea fans congregate.

Outside the Stamford Bridge gates, supporters wait to meet friends.

Police frisk fans at the entrance to the stadium

now. It is the extra people going who are making the difference and the extra people going are probably the more middle-class people, the more typical Fulham middle-class individual. The body of support in the bad old days when it was really quite violent and the club weren't so successful has remained much the same. I think it is the increase in numbers among the more fickle fans who tend to be more middle class. That would be my guess.

'The distinctive hooligan element that causes us the most difficulty don't go to the matches. They are a problem for us outside. Where they hang out is the thousand dollar question. They will normally be anywhere from central London, Euston, Victoria or the pubs around here.

'We categorise fans as A, B and C. A is a normal supporter and no problem. B is a type of supporter, who, if there is trouble, will probably get involved. C is the type who organises or orchestrates and will get involved from the outset in violence. If we are talking about Category C hooligans for Chelsea, there's probably 150 names that we are aware of and of those twenty-five are active, but active is difficult to define.

'Some of them went to Seville, for instance, for the Cup Winners' Cup game against Real Betis, but did not cause any trouble. They tend to only respond to challenges from other people. The best, the most professional – these are all the wrong terms – will only react to someone of a similar stature really in terms of organising violence.

'They get no fulfilment out of beating up a bobble hat. What they seek to do is to challenge their compatriots from the other Premiership clubs. If their compatriots do not turn up, then they don't get involved. If they are challenged or confronted, they will never give ground but they are not seeking to have a go at someone who will demean their repu-tation. They will sometimes meet at railway stations but generally they will give each other a ring on their mobiles and say they will meet at Putney Bridge. They can have a bit of a battle there and then go on somewhere else.

'It is a very strange world. If one defines a criminal as someone who has got a criminal record, then most of them are criminals but they also normally have jobs that could be any type of job. There is a bit of a fallacy going around that they are all stock-brokers.

'We cope with them by overtly policing them. We know who they are, we have their photographs and we follow them around. They know we follow them around. They will speak to us. My spotters and I went to Seville and they went up to them. Some-times they nod at them, sometimes they threaten them, sometimes they have a conversation and they know we are there. We get in their face.

'We have a governmental agreement with other European partners that if a European club is being visited by an English club and the local police wish us to help them in advice and identification, then we will help them, and we did that in Norway, Slovakia and Spain this year.

'There are a few pubs that they regularly go to but they very rarely cause a problem. There is Rosie's outside the stadium and that gets an enormous amount of noise and chanting which is risqué. If you have seen the size of the landlord, no one ever argues with him. It is just a football pub. It has not got a bad reputation. It is well managed and generally the guys we are talking about will sit in it and not cause any problems.

'In terms of our preparation and planning, the Cup match against Man United caused us the most problems. In terms of actual problems, it was probably the Coca-Cola Cup game against Arsenal.

In the tunnel Stamford the Lion hugs a young mascot.

The ball boys get ready to lead the team out.

The waiting is over, now it's time to produce. Expectant fans look on as the players emerge onto the pitch.

The Arsenal fans started to leave early and started to cause a bit of trouble in Fulham Road. It was fairly easily contained. There was a bit of damage to stalls in Fulham Road, and there was a bit of coin-throwing from the Chelsea fans into the Arsenal fans. But generally we have had a pretty good year.

'We work closely with the club and the local authority although the aims of the club have to be slightly different to ours. The local authority wants a safe event and the club wants a safe event but it wants to make lots of money, too. That sometimes conflicts with us. When we have had disagreements we have been able to come to some amicable solution. Either we have compromised or they have given in to me. They gave into me on things like sale of tickets and licensing hours for the bars because they do not want to be in a position of disorder.

'Our strategy is to prevent disorder, we want to provide a safe event, we want to minimise the disruption to the local community. Obviously, the first two are interlinked. Disruption to the local community is a difficult one because when you get 35,000 people coming out of the ground on a Saturday evening it does cause some disruption, you cannot get around that. They won't have Chelsea and Fulham playing on the same day. Once we get it, there is also a rule that says all matches on the same day should kick off at the same time. If we have an early start and West Ham are playing later, the hooligans can arrange to meet. Whereas if we have the game at 3pm and they have their game at 3pm generally they can't meet. It doesn't happen very often. There were three incidents with Chelsea fans away from this division. There are distinct groups within the Chelsea Category Cs. They talk to each other but they don't necessarily mix.

'We decide in advance what the category of the match is going to be. 'A' is no problem, not expect-ing any difficulty, just lots of people. It is all based on intelligence, what we know people are likely to do, what happened in previous matches. 'B' is that there is some potential but we are not expecting anything too difficult. 'C' is where there is potential for real disorder and issues about public safety.

'This year, Chelsea have only had one Category 'C' and that was Chelsea v Man United. As it turned out, it was an early start, we kept them in the West Stand, Man United got the result they wanted, it was pouring with rain, it was a non-starter. Historically, though, they are not keen on each other. There is another issue to that because there are the Cockney Reds who are the London-based United supporters and they always like to have a bit of a bunfight.

'Looking back on it, we might have made the Arsenal game a 'C' and the United game a 'B'. As the season wears on, if Chelsea start doing badly, attendance drops and the Category 'C' hooligans lose interest, then we might downgrade certain matches. Having said that, if they do well, there are big crowds and sometimes there is a history of fighting between certain teams. That can happen if they get someone in the Cup that they used to fight but they are not in the same league now, like Millwall. If Millwall come to Chelsea that would be Category 'C'.

'Once we have decided the category, that triggers a response. If it is an 'A' it is 40 police to cover it, 'B' is 60 and perhaps 120 for a 'C' plus dogs and horses. The number of dogs and horses will change. If it is an 'A' we do not need to police inside the ground, theoretically, that is all done by Chelsea stewards. If it is a 'C', we put more in. We would police the perimeter of the ground, areas like Fulham Broadway and Fulham Road. The gates are normally the main areas we police but we have to be vigilant everywhere.'

Chelsea fans at the Maze prison wait to watch the match on television.

Pitch side passion: the referee cautions Real Betis's coach during the tense Cup Winners' Cup game. The coach was eventually escorted from the ground by the police.

Michael Duberry seeks guidance from Graham Rix during a stormy clash with Leeds.

FOR THE PLAYERS, LIKE THE POLICE, preparation often is everything. It is the unseen work, the intelligence, the attention to detail, that makes the difference when the big teams come to the Bridge. They may not put the opposition in quite such finite categories but they know when the real tests are around the corner.

After the game, the atmosphere in the dressing room often can be strangely muted, as though they are all spent, totally physically and emotionally drained. Again, you get the invigorating feeling of seeing men who have given everything for their club. Sit in the Chelsea dressing room after a match and you will never again subscribe to the view that many modern-day footballers just go through the motions, that they do not give their all for their club. It is not true at Chelsea.

Only twice this season was there an air of utter elation in the dressing room after the game. The first was following the emotional night of Vialli's first match in charge when they produced a Herculean effort to get past Arsenal in the Coca-Cola Cup semi-final second leg and ensured another trip to Wembley. There was champagne spraying in the dressing room that night and whooping and yelling and all the things you would expect of an archetypal celebratory scene. They seemed to realise that much of the rest of their season hinged on that game.

The other occasion was a more obvious one, the victory over VfB Stuttgart in the Cup Winners' Cup Final at Rasunda Stadium in Stockholm. People made and salvaged their reputations that night and there was unrestrained joy in that dressing room as well.

Even that night, though, by the time they got back on the team coach, they were subdued. By the time they got on the plane taking them back to Heathrow in the early hours and sat down next

to their wives, they were positively withdrawn. Wise stood up midway through that flight and said that the team were going to sing a song for the rest of the plane. Only Frank Leboeuf stood up to join him so the song had to be abandoned.

After other games, when you would have expected elation, there was none. It was relatively quiet, for instance, after the Coca-Cola Cup Final save for Neil Barnett being dragged fully clothed into the huge bath in the Wembley changing room as he was trying to conduct a radio interview. It was quiet, too, after the Cup Winners' Cup semi-final victory over Vicenza.

'After the game, it's a funny time,' Oz says, 'especially if they lose. They just take their kit off and the YTS would get rid of it quickly. But you don't rush them, you know. They might sit there for twenty minutes, just speechless. It looks a bit chaotic after the game.'

For the physios, the after-match is often the busiest part of the day. 'The first thing you do,' Byrne says 'is treat any injuries that have occurred during the game and assess any damage. You have also got to make sure that they reload their carbohydrates. We use Lucozade as a glucose drink and we use a powder carbohydrate called Maxim which restores glycogen. They have a post-match rub to remove lactic acid from the muscles, the thing that makes you feel stiff.'

When the team travel to games, of course, the routine changes. For the furthest domestic away games, such as Newcastle United, Leeds United and Manchester United, they fly from Heathrow. For closer away games, even games on the other side of London such as Arsenal or Spurs, they travel by coach.

The seating on the coach usually corresponds to who they mix with the most. The younger players, the players who have come up through the ranks, lads such as Jody Morris, Duberry, Sinclair and Newton, all sit together, either engrossed in their Play Stations, listening to music or chatting and laughing with each other.

They can be long, boring journeys, slogging up the M1 or the M6 to Coventry and Birmingham. Sometimes, they are enlivened by supporters with their scarves flapping out of their windows driving alongside and honking their horns in greetings and encouragement. Usually, they are featureless and dull, a means to an end, the quickest, easiest method of getting from A to B.

Some of them play cards, some listen to music. The Italian players usually sit together talking. Dennis Wise and Steve Clarke will have a game of cards together. Mark Hughes is one who likes to sit and read. It changes from trip to trip. Chelsea is not one of those clubs divided into definite, separate cliques.

The travel arrangements for these domestic trips is one of the many tasks performed by Gwyn Williams. The logistics of getting a squad of players from A to B is a feat in itself and the notice of all the times when players must report to Harlington or Stamford Bridge to catch the bus is pinned up on the notice board at Harlington days in advance. Usually, it is written in big, black capital letters so there can be no excuses.

At hotels, the habit of players sharing rooms, which one might think would have become an anachronism in these days of super-rich clubs who could surely spare the price of a few extra single rooms, continues unbroken. It helps to combat loneliness and stops players burning the midnight oil when they should be resting. If they stay up, they keep their teammate up too, and incur his wrath.

The more solitary among the players, men such as Graeme Le Saux, who likes to occupy himself with a book, are allowed to have their own room if they want it but most have grown up with the tradition of sharing. At Chelsea, Wise shares with Clarke., Mark Hughes with Hitchcock, Flo with De Goey, Newton with Sinclair, Duberry with Morris, Petrescu with Poyet.

The same arrangements usually apply whatever sort of team trip they go on. In January, they spent four days in the Algarve by way of a winter break, a recharging of batteries after the disaster of the 5–3 FA Cup third round defeat to Manchester United at Stamford Bridge which had sapped morale and caused more doubts about Gullit's regime.

After one night of high spirits, Gullit found it necessary to issue a warning to the players to behave more responsibly but the rest of the trip was like a sportsman's idyll, four days of swimming, golfing, tennis and horse riding. Zola, just as he practises his free-kicks incessantly at Harlington, was the model of application on the practice range, honing his pitching obsessively while many of the others larked around.

Part of Gullit's intention in taking the squad on such a trip was to try to bond the disparate elements together. Jim Smith, the Derby County manager, has talked eloquently in the past of the difficulties of forging real team spirit at a club if there are too many foreign players who cannot communicate well with the rest of their teammates and tend to keep themselves to themselves when they leave for home after training.

Part of Arsenal's success last season was due to the fact that the French and the Dutch players mixed so easily with the English rump of the team. It was clear to everyone how hard they all fought for each other. Team spirit is something that is easily overlooked but it often can be the crucial missing ingredient that costs a team dearly.

Team training Algarve style. Ade Mafe puts the players through their paces as autograph hunters hover on the touchline.

The players find their own way to relax during the mid–season break in Portugal: a game of chess for Dennis Wise and Mike Banks, while the perfectionist Zola hones chipping skills of a different kind.

Di Matteo finds a moment of solitude by the pool and Le Saux and Wise try horse riding.

The Business

MICHAEL HERD, A FORMER SPORTS editor of the *London Evening Standard*, and still a respected columnist on the paper, is a master of the art of telling lovely stories. He has got one for most people and almost all of them are incisive and instructive. His Ken Bates story is no exception. Somehow, it gets right to the core of the man.

Having at some time in the past been introduced to a gathering by the Chelsea chairman as Michael Turd, Herd was aware that one of his *Standard* colleagues had just been described as a 'talentless cretin and a gutless coward' by Bates, so he wrote in his column that any man scared of the bully should imagine him wearing only jockey shorts.

Bates is nothing if not bloody-minded. It probably is his defining characteristic, the thing that has made him such an outstandingly successful businessman. He saw the piece and promptly stripped off, strode out on to the pitch and had his picture taken. It was published in the club magazine alongside a forthright challenge for Herd to do the same. He looked in the mirror and admitted defeat.

It is hard to get the better of Ken Bates. That almost could be his epitaph. You can forget his faults, really. He has got them in spades like the rest of us. He can be rude, offhand, he can make you feel small when he wants to. But he is not a monster, he is not even a bad man. His ends justify his means. What he has achieved for Chelsea Football Club, every supporter should be grateful for.

Sometimes, the supporters want to love him because they know he saved the club. Sometimes they want to hate him because he hoists up the season-ticket prices. Sometimes, they remind themselves that although Hoddle and Gullit and Vialli have restored Chelsea's fortunes on the pitch, they could not have done it without the backing Bates gave them. Sometimes, like the time he sacked Gullit, they think he has overstepped the mark.

I had an open-necked shirt on the first time I met him in the informal reception area of the old club offices before they moved to the swish new premises on the other side of The Shed. 'Oliver,' he said, with mock formality, 'What a nice tie you've got on today.' The shame of it was, I actually looked down to try to study the object of his approbation.

When I danced my way around a question, struggling inarticulately with it, coming at it from several different angles, getting no closer to a conclusion, he seized his chance. 'You're not very good at this sort of thing are you?' he said. I had to agree with him. He made me laugh anyway. If you try to take him on, then you find the conversation over pretty soon. If you play along, he can be engaging company. If you do not take offence too easily, you get on fine with Ken Bates.

In many ways, he is a bully, a confrontational speaker and arguer who prides himself, in fact, on being rude. 'I'm off back to my pigsty,' Bates said once after a meeting of Premier League chairmen. 'You meet a better class of person there.' People have to take him as he is. If they don't like it, he doesn't care. He's made his money himself, so why should he mind who he offends?

Part of you – the professional part in my case – rails at him for the way he treats the written media who do so much to promote the image of Chelsea every year, who help to spread news of Chelsea's triumphs around the globe. The press box, to the shame of others at the club but to the almost perversely stubborn delight of the chairman, is the worst in the FA Carling Premiership. It is cramped, almost devoid of power points and so low in the stand that the view of play is obscured when supporters stand up in front or on either side.

Ken Bates dons his hard hat to tour the building site.

Work in progress at the
McDonalds-sponsored family
enclosure.

As evening draws in, dinner
is served from one of the
many burger trucks.

But there is a part, too, that warms to him and admires him more every time you meet him. He deserves respect for the way he treats people the same way. His refusal to be conned by flattery rather flies in the face of the inferiority complex theory and there are other redeeming features, too. His skin is not quite as thick as he would have you believe, and he sets a high value on common courtesies which are not necessarily visible in his own public conduct but take on great importance for him in private.

It is impossible not to admire what he has done for Chelsea, too. When you wander around Stamford Bridge today, it is almost as though you are looking at the prototype of a modern football club, the sort of thing the planners might have envisaged in their wildest dreams twenty years ago but which has not really come to fruition anywhere else.

The vision of Bates and some of the executives he has brought in to help him has turned Chelsea from a struggling middle-of-the-road club into a thoroughly modern organisation that now has the infrastructure to provide the resources to keep Chelsea challenging the very best in the Premiership for years to come. Bates has adapted to these needs, seized these initiatives, where other, younger men conspicuously have failed. Where the limit of others' ambitions has been to tack a branch of Safeway or Kwik Save on to the back of the main stand and call the stadium an entertainment complex, Bates has done the thing in style, with a luxury hotel (others in football are fond of calling it the Bates Motel), four restaurants and a night club flanking the football pitch. There are plans for a giant health club, too, and in time the stadium's own railway station.

He took a group of us round what was then a building site in late July last year before the 1997/98 season had begun. He wore a yellow hard hat and helped us pick our way under ladders and over rubble, pointing out in great detail what was going to be where, how grand a scale the whole project was being built upon and how it was going to put Chelsea out in front.

Six months later, some time in January, I took the tour again. They were almost preparing for opening this time and Bates was, if anything, even more effusive. The Galleria, the corporate entertainment rooms that look out on to the pitch from behind giant glass windows where The Shed used to be, could hold this many tennis courts, he said. He explained the new hi-tech ticket office system, too, that records everyone's voice as they try to buy their chance to see a future game, and he talked his way through the menus in each of the restaurants. His hand was in everything.

He found time, too, to mock the way football used to be, to deride the old standards that he realised quicker than most were no longer acceptable to the new breed of moneyed supporter who has come to represent Chelsea's staple diet. The new ethos at Stamford Bridge is about catering, literally and figuratively, for this new wave of fans.

'I do not believe this country is poverty-stricken,' Bates said. 'I think that is exaggerated by people who have a vested interest in running their charities and being self-important. No doubt there are some poor people just as there are affluent people. Working-class people, and I am one, have drifted away from Spain and Majorca and are going on seven-day cruises to the Caribbean or Greece or Turkey.

'As the standard of living increases, so they want better facilities and they are entitled to them. I don't see anybody wanting to go to the cinema, standing in the rain, with their coat collar turned up, eating a pork pie, watching a film. They expect to go into centrally heated cinemas, sit in tip-up seats and be able to buy a whole range of food and drinks.

'The old joke was that we thought we ought to maintain The Shed in some form because it was an institution like the Kop at Anfield or the Shelf at Spurs. So we decided to call one of the bars at the ground The Shed. So when we were considering the interior decorating, I was tempted to do a crumbling concrete floor, rusting corrugated iron sheets on the walls and a blocked toilet in the corner. But then I thought "no, to hell with tradition".

'The old idea at football would be that people came to the game at quarter to three because there is nothing else to do. You might as well sit in the pub with a jar. Well, we have got 20 per cent more than the official recommendation of toilets, we have paid particular attention to the ladies. If they get proper facilities they will come. We are the first club to have put a ladies' toilet in the press room.

'We are improving the quality of the food. We have got our own TV channel which runs from 11.30 to 6.30 so the ordinary guy can now watch Channel Chelsea, so people can stay later, watch the manager's press conference live and avoid the rush to get out, and maybe the tubes are half empty by then. We are providing a full range of facilities. Just because we are working class does not mean you have to have a pie and a pint. Is there a working class any more anyway? They all seem to be computer mechanics or telephone technicians. You have got rid of coal mines, factories and shipyards. Times are changing.'

In many ways, Bates has taken the football dream to its limit by placing the club at the very centre of a whole host of other outlets, by building something that puts even some of the great European clubs to shame in its logistical planning. There is a great symbolism in the fact that he has created all these fashionable eateries and elegant hotel rooms but ensured that at its centre is a plain football pitch. He may be a multi-millionaire now but football is the

centre of his world and he deserves our affection for that, too.

It might have been Hillary Rodham Clinton, America's First Lady, who first opined that 'it takes a village' but it was Ken Bates, Chelsea's first chairman, who had the nous and the guts to build it. It is all around him now, like a great monument to him and his club. Since earlier this year, when he decamped from his seventeen-acre farm in Beaconsfield with his girlfriend, Suzannah, for the penthouse on the top floor of the hotel complex, he lives at Chelsea, sleeps at Chelsea and eats at Chelsea. It is his home town, his Saturday afternoon, his dinner party venue, his local, his corner shop, his everything. If for nothing else, he should be revered for the transformation he has wrought, for the concept he has grasped. Love him or hate him, he is showing the rest the way forward.

HIS OLD OFFICE CARRIED a few more signposts to his personality. Just as everyone who ever visits Alex Ferguson's manager's room at Manchester United's training ground at The Cliff always notices the sign on the wall that says HACUMFIGOVAN, a doff of the cap to his Glasgow upbringing, and the pictures on the cabinet of Ferguson with Sir Matt Busby, or Ferguson with Jack Charlton, so Bates's old office was cluttered with the memorabilia of stardust memories and paeans to his homespun philosophies.

In no particular order, there was a framed article from t he *Independent* on the wall whose headline described Bates as 'The Maverick James Anderton of Football', a comparison with the former Chief Constable of Greater Manchester Police that obviously pleased Bates. Anderton had a big, bushy beard, too, and a similarly forthright approach.

There was an action shot of Kerry Dixon, a picture of Bobby Campbell, a letter from John Major, a pic-

Ken Bates works with
his personal assistant in
his homely Stamford Bridge
office and (below) admires
the development of his
penthouse suite in
the hotel.

ture of the Norwegian ambassador at Stamford Bridge. An England shirt hung next to that, donated by a former player. Then there was an article with a headline proclaiming 'Hoddle plots United's downfall'.

There was a picture of Bates with Hoddle, a picture of Dixon with David Speedie, a group of caricatures of Bates and various pictures of family pets and relatives.

One of the centrepieces of the office was a handsome, low wooden table that Bates had got for a steal – like many rich men, he loves a bargain. It had been hand-made by Indian villagers. 'I'd rather have that than something out of Habitat,' he said. Then there was a poem on the wall, Bates' equivalent of having Rudyard Kipling's 'If' up there. It went like this:

If you think you are beaten, you are,
If you think you dare not, you don't,
If you want to win but think you can't,
It's almost a hunch you won't,
If you think you'll lose, you're lost,
If you're frightened of the world, you'll find
Success begins with a person's will,
It's all in a state of mind.

Next to that, there was another elongated slogan that one can only think Bates must have attached importance to, so prominent was its placing. The writing was striking in its bold black letters. It said: 'Life's battles don't always go to the stronger or better person but sooner or later the person who wins is the person who thinks he or she can.'

BATES TOOK OVER AT CHELSEA IN 1982 WHEN the club were losing £12,000 a week and were fast declining after the end of the glory years of the Seventies. When the new chairman took charge there seemed to be little hope for the future, just fond memories of a stylish but under-achieving past that most thought would never be recreated.

Bates has an intriguing background, not quite mired in the same sort of mystery as that of the Formula One supremo, Bernie Ecclestone, but with the same exotic feel to it, the same smell of success. He had grown sugar in Australia, entered the construction business in South Africa, reclaimed land in the West Indies and founded a bank in Ireland. He had invested in a sand and gravel business in Lancashire, lived for a while in Monte Carlo and been chairman of Oldham Athletic.

At Chelsea, his early years were spent battling to buy the Stamford Bridge grounds which were not owned by the football club, so that the club could regain control of its destiny. For a decade, it seemed he was firefighting, struggling against problems, rather than being able to create anything positive. Even though there was continuing scepticism about him in these years, he saved the club from bankruptcy and it is his decisions that put the club in the increasingly pre-eminent position they find themselves in today.

'I took over in '82,' Bates said, 'and until we got the ground, until we were secure in the stadium, everything stemmed from that. We could not get the finances to build a stadium on a piece of land that wasn't ours and at the same time some Irish idiot was banging on about the fact that he was going to throw us out.

'All the time, we were spending our time fighting to stay at Stamford Bridge. We achieved that in December 1992. Although we had been doing a few things like refurbishing the east stand and taking a punt on the fact that we were going to be here anyway, we were taking a risk. 15 December 1992, when we won the battle to stay, that meant we could start putting our plans into action.

'Taking Glenn Hoddle on as the manager was the first stage of us stating our intentions of being one of

The back of the old club shop gets a final walk
past as fans buy tickets from portakabins.
This is soon to go.

Putting final touches to
the Megastore.

Shops, restaurants and
a grandstand sprout from
the west side.

the élite, and Hoddle took us from the mediocrity of being mid-table to the start of being a serious challenger. If you think about it, under Hoddle our league positions in his years in charge were eleventh, fourteenth, eleventhth. But he got us to an FA Cup final and a semi-final and he introduced a change in policy.

'He had lived in Monaco, he had always been a thinker anyway and an intellectual and he had wanted to play the beautiful game as it should be played, beautifully. He started trying to teach the players he had around him to play his way. Mark Hughes was a great signing and so was Gullit. So we had made a start. Glenn started making people think about the way they treat their bodies and their attitude to the game.

'Having got the ground, then we started to get the income stream. Hoddle got the gates up which increased our takings so we got better sponsorship and all we have done is put it back in the team. There are other clubs who neglect development and put it into the team, others who neglect the team and put it to development, but I have always said the two go hand in hand. Unless you want to be a nine-day wonder you have to build the income streams capable of sustaining a great team and that is what we have done. We don't pay silly money and in the modern context we are not big spenders *per se*. What we do do is pay good wages and frankly I don't have a problem with that. We are now in the entertainment business and most entertainers are very well paid. That is the same in football. The average player has only seven or eight years at the top. When they are thirty-five or whatever, they have to go to Millwall and compete with people who have been doing it for twenty years already. They have to avoid the fact that the world owes them a living because they scored a goal twenty years ago.

'Our goal now is to be among the European élite, it is as simple as that. We are slowly but surely getting there. We have won two trophies this season alone and we are in Europe again. We want more than our fair share of pots. Our ambition is to match Manchester United. We have done it in one respect – we have both lost 3–2 away at Coventry City.

'They get crowds of 55,000, we only have 40,000. But we are in a much more fashionable area which means we can attract a more cosmopolitan crowd and tourists. We have got a hotel, sports and leisure centre and a megastore. It is revolutionary in design. This year we are looking for £7 to £8 million from the Megastore and the problem we have is getting the stuff because Umbro have to plan a year ahead and they did not expect it to be such a big success.

'We have launched a mail order firm now, too. We sent out 14,000 parcels in December. We are on the Internet now. We are ploughing money back into research and development. We are going to have our own beer and spirits, our own wine. But everything we do, it will have to be the best. We are building it all the time. An awful lot of people here have got nothing to do with football.

'I used to have this philosophy at Oldham. I said the club has to be wealthy enough to withstand the setbacks that come with a bad season. Even if you have a bad season in the Premiership, you have got your television money and your sponsorship so it is not as black and white as it was thirty years ago. But nevertheless if we have got a situation where the football club has not got the money to buy a player, then the rest of the group has to be able to help it out if necessary.'

So far, it has all worked like a dream for Bates, personally and professionally. His own fortune has multiplied in tandem with that of the club. His 19 per cent share of Chelsea Village is worth more than

£32 million, and he is also believed to exercise influence over two trusts which account for a further £39 million. He does not deny that Chelsea has made him even richer than he already was. But he says the money is not his motivation and when you see him at football grounds all around the country week in and week out, when you see him at every European ground Chelsea visit, the fact that he is a genuine football man shines through.

'It has made me richer. I have been the full-time chairman for sixteen years but who knows how much money I would have made out of something else? For ten years I did not take a penny out. Even when I did start paying myself, at £120,000 a year, it is still far less than many others.

'Every football supporter in the country would like to run their own club because they think they can do it better than the prat who is running it now. I have become a prat if you like. I am a supporter who is running a football club and I love it. It is a way of life. It is a way to make things happen, to get things done, to improve things. I am a bit of a crusader. Through this, I am also on the FA council. I am a bit of a maverick there but at least you can get things done. It is a soap box but that is not the reason why I am here today. I find it annoying that you get rung up to be asked things that are nothing to do with you just because you are the chairman of Chelsea.'

IF THE MAJORITY OF BATES'S TIME OF LATE has been spent overseeing developments at Chelsea Village, he was, inevitably, deeply involved in the raging controversy surrounding the departure of Gullit in February. Many blamed Bates's own ego for the end of a reign that had brought so much attention and glamour back to the club. His detractors thought that Bates simply could not stand the fact that Gullit, a larger than life personality, was becoming Chelsea's front man instead of him.

The reality is a little different. There may have been some unspoken tension between Bates and Gullit over their respective profiles but if there was, it never surfaced into open hostility and it certainly was not decisive. A month before he was sacked, Bates was still talking fondly about Gullit and scoffing dismissively at any suggestions he might not sign a new contract with the club, something that had long been mooted in the popular press.

It was mid-January when I first spoke to him about the situation. In the light of what happened and the accusations of greed that were later levelled at the Dutchman, there is a certain bitter-sweet quality about some of Bates's praise for him when he was still in charge. Much has been made of the chairman saying he did not expect Gullit to go to Peterborough on a wet Monday night in the middle of winter but his support for his managerial *modus operandi* extended beyond that.

'Gullit's attitude is extremely unconventional,' Bates said then. 'But when Hoddle left and Gullit took the job he put into practice his attitude and his way of life. It is significant of the man that he could have gone to a club in Japan for the same money we are paying him and had what would have amounted to a holiday.

'He could have been a giant among pygmies. But he preferred to come here for the challenge of proving he had another future in coaching. And his attitude was quite simple. He chose to play his squad system and he said nobody was guaranteed a place and that did not sit well with some people.

'I get on very well with Ruud. We have got a very similar sense of humour. We have a directors' car park and I came in one day and somebody had parked in my place. So I went in to lunch and I said

For the last fifty years Annette Flood has observed the antics of Chelsea players and fans from the window of her Chelsea flat. Her view of the Stamford Bridge pitch will soon be blocked by the new development.

to him, "I'm very proud of what you're doing and I'll back you all the way but you've parked in my space. Don't ever do that again". And he just burst out laughing. I'm not star struck. I do not find it necessary to go out to have meals with my players and eat with them. I leave that to other, lesser mortals. Ruud's his own man and I respect that.'

That respect soon disappeared, though, when Bates and Hutchinson grew tired of what they saw as unacceptable stalling by Gullit over discussions for a new contract. The existing one was due to run out in the summer of 1998 and they were growing nervous that they might be left in the lurch again just as they had been caught out when Hoddle left to take up the England job.

The crisis was precipitated when Bates and Hutchinson realised just how much money Gullit was demanding. It was the kind of pay-packet that would have made him far and away the highest-paid manager in the country. Bates began to think he was being taken for a ride and the bloody mindedness took over again.

IT WAS NOT AN AMICABLE SPLIT. IT WAS acrimonious and lastingly so. The parting of the ways came on Thursday 12 February but the recriminations were still rumbling on in April. A series of articles garnered from Gullit's autobiography were published in the *Daily Mirror* and Bates felt the need to reply to them in his programme notes.

'My attention has been drawn to articles written by Ruud Gullit in a downmarket tabloid,' Bates wrote. 'I think it really sad that he has so demeaned himself, he has let himself down by showing in public a side of his character that everybody was aware of but kept quiet about. I can only repeat what I have said before. We tried to renew his contract as far back as last October but he consistently stalled.

'Near the end, it transpired that he was delaying because of his own personal problems that had nothing to do with Chelsea. Colin Hutchinson was sympathetic but it got to the stage when Chelsea's interest had to come first. He didn't go due to pressure from the City because unlike Newcastle we don't have City types controlling our finances or sitting on the Board. He went because Colin Hutchinson wasn't prepared to pay a huge percentage of his player budget for a part-time playboy manager who carried out his lucrative commercial contracts at the expense of his training – that much was obvious to everybody in his last game at Highbury.

'Ruud was a very successful manager. He is part of Chelsea's history and his portrait still hangs in the Shed Bar. He has only let himself down – nobody else. Since he is now between jobs perhaps he can now find time to sit down and pen a letter of thanks for the special present that Suzannah bought Estelle when she had her baby before last Christmas. After all, Judy Walker, who works in our office, did.'

The bile spewed out by both men meant Bates transferred his affections quickly to the new man in charge. Vialli, you feel instinctively, might be more Bates's kind of manager. Quieter, more reflective than Gullit, he has the profile necessary to attract big-name players without the fondness for the show-business kind of publicity that his predecessor had begun to wallow in.

It is hard, for example, to see Vialli appearing on *An Audience with Elton John* as Gullit did. It is hard to see him being canvassed for his opinion on great intellectual matters as Gullit was, hard to see him becoming a television personality as Gullit did. But he is qualified for these things. In many ways he is more qualified, more articulate and intelligent than the man he supplanted. It is just not his style to project himself in the same way.

Even before Vialli had managed to squeeze Chelsea into the Cup Winners' Cup Final, Bates was eulogising his new man. 'Luca and I have something big in common,' he said. 'Get things done, win things, achieve. We gave him the job because we thought he was the right man at the right time at this club.

'Immediately, he was put under pressure, unfair pressure. There was talk of a dressing-room split between him and Ruud. A dressing-room revolt with the players. People asked whether he was the right man for the job. And it was suggested I had Terry Venables waiting in the wings to take over.

'All of it was untrue and unfair on Luca. The Venables thing particularly annoyed me. It seems people still like to try to unsettle Chelsea, me if you like. Luca has simply put his head down and got on with the job. I have been impressed with the way he has handled himself.

'When he makes a decision, he explains it. When he drops a player, he tells him why. He doesn't just pin up the team and let players read whether they are in or out. There are no shocks and it is simple man-management. He will also admit when he makes mistakes. At Leeds the other night, he realised he had got things wrong and held his hands up. I would say Luca has kept his head when under a great deal of pressure. He is a nice bloke, an honest man and, of course, we hope he makes a huge success of this. We are ambitious, so is he and that can only be a good partnership.'

The partnership on the playing side extends beyond Bates and Vialli. If Bates still wields the real power, some of it has been delegated to Hutchinson, his right-hand man and the executive who, on paper at least, has responsibility for the football club, particularly when it comes to the purchase of new players.

His separate role, originally created as a pragmatic device to try to stop the late Matthew Harding interfering in the running of team affairs and sabotaging the strict code of secrecy that Chelsea adopt in their transfer dealings, has grown as Bates has devoted some of his energies to Chelsea Village.

Hutchinson is an unsmiling man who appears to have a permanent scowl on his face. In many ways, he is the conduit between Bates and the staff at Harlington. If a transfer is to be done, he flies out to wherever he needs to go to start negotiations. When Vialli and Graham Rix draw up a list of players they would like to recruit, it is Hutchinson who goes about trying to recruit them. With Gwyn Williams, they represent a formidable quartet.

Rix explained succinctly how the system works. 'Colin will put pressure on Luca and say "Who do you want? Draw me up a list of what you need." Then Luca will sit down with me and Gwyn. We say what are our priorities if money is no object. Who do we really like? We draw up a list of three or four in each position and say "There you are, in an ideal world". Schmeichel, Desailly, those sort of people. We do not want somebody coming in who is going to be a bad influence on people, not train properly.

'We want good strong solid characters like Gustavo Poyet. Great example. Me and Gwyn went to watch him play for Zaragoza in 1997 against Real Madrid. He was in a poor team and they got absolutely hammered but from the first minute to the last he was wanting to play, getting hold of his teammates and you could see he was a good strong character. Obviously we still want to produce our own. I would like eight or nine homegrown players and two superstars. That would be the icing on the cake.

'But we have to be careful to balance it off. We

The fans of the future: Ken Bates with young Chelsea fans in the Megastore.

An obsession passed on through generations: young fan Connor Hart makes a visit to his neighbour's garden shed, a shrine to Chelsea Football Club.

want to attract young kids to the club but they have to see that if they do come to Chelsea they have a chance of playing in the first team. If there's a school-boy here and he's twelve or thirteen years of age and he's got to choose between us and Arsenal, I tell Luca that we want him, then he will go over and make a fuss of him and little things like that. He is not just interested in the first team.'

IF HUTCHINSON, WILLIAMS AND RIX represent the power structure beneath Bates at the football club, there is a different pyramid at Chelsea Village. The football club is still run by football people because they know football best. Chelsea Village is run by businessmen because they know business best. 'Ian Hutchinson, one of our former players, used to be the commercial manager here in 1979,' Bates said. 'Well, he might have had the greatest long throw in football but I don't think he knew much about business. We have now got a guy who used to work for Andrew Lloyd Webber in charge of merchandising. We headhunt these people. We go for the top people in their fields.'

Chelsea Village still has football at its heart but someone such as Ian Hutchinson would be lost in the myriad concerns it now entails. There is the Megastore, the biggest in the Premiership, the four restaurants, the four star hotel, the mail order firm, a travel agent. It goes on and on and it gets bigger and bigger. And as the money rolls in, the purchasing power of the football club increases.

The Megastore is the biggest money earner. It is spread over 10,500 square feet and employs fifty people at peak times. Match days represent only a fifth of sales. It sells scent, clothes, earrings, baby clothes. You can smell of Chelsea, wear Chelsea, pierce yourself with Chelsea, eat out of Chelsea lunch boxes, drink out of Chelsea mugs, ride to work or school on Chelsea mountain bikes. In here, Chelsea really is life.

On the way in, shoppers are greeted by two huge pictures of Vialli at the entrance, one holding the Coca-Cola Cup. There are Chelsea number-plates in the window and a giant Dennis Wise head. T-shirts proclaim 'There's only one team in Europe' and next to them mountain bikes are set up with wheels painted like footballs.

There are hats, balls, flags, shorts and more types of polo shirts than you can imagine. A Chelsea 50cc scooter is £2,500. On the second floor there are videos playing of Chelsea winning the Coca-Cola Cup as you go up the escalator. In a cabinet, there are Chelsea watches, gold and silver pennants, rings and cufflinks.

On racks on another wall, there are Seventies shirts, team wear, babies' bibs, babies' mittens, wall clocks, duvet covers, dressing gowns, towels, birthday cards. *Ruud Gullit's Chelsea Diary* has been reduced to £5. Downstairs, in another section, there is a television showing the Saturday afternoon scores. There are bottles, wristbands, cuddly toys, lunch boxes, frying pans, a CFC Harley Davidson motorbike for £20,000, bras and briefs, and the CFC One fragrance for men and women. It is all a far cry from the original club shop that operated from a small room on Fulham Road.

Then there is the Chelsea Village Hotel, the imposing edifice that dominates the stadium now. The brochure goes for all the buzz words. It says it is 'contemporary, cosmopolitan, stylish', that it has 'traditional comforts in a modern and unconventional setting'.

It also has 160 guest rooms equpped with voice mail messaging and data points for computer modems. The cost is £125 for an executive single, and £155 for a superior double. Add to that the four

While the Chelsea Village is transformed, on the Fulham Road one of the fans' favourite old haunts, The Lost Café, remains the same.

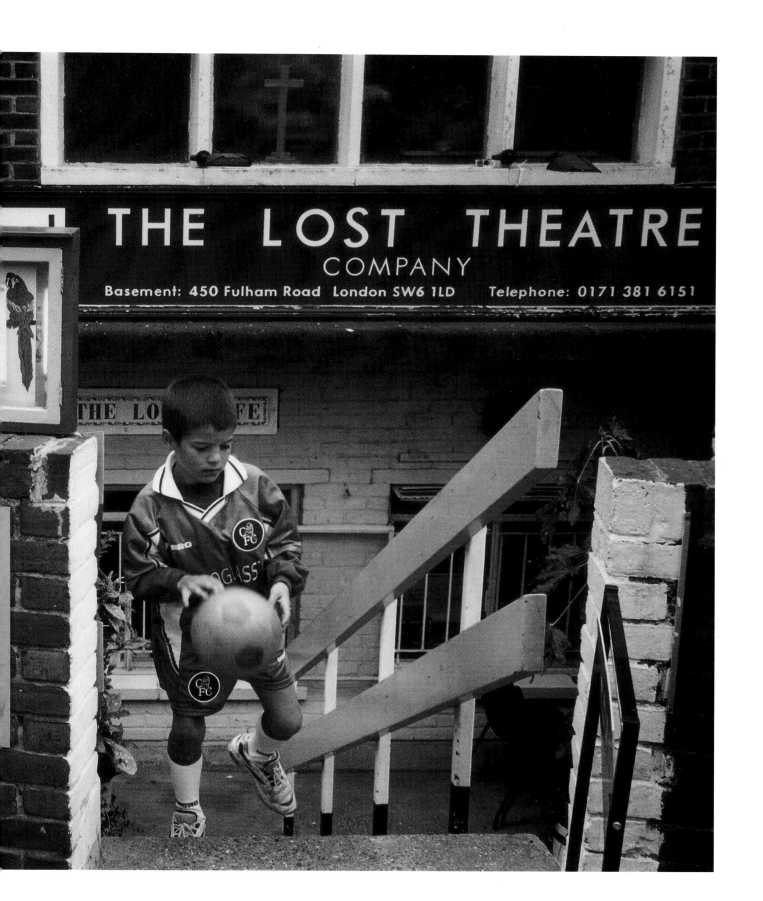

restaurants, two bars, business centre, underground parking, meetings and exhibition space for 1500 and you have just about said it all. And from the top floor, with the Monet prints at your back, you get a lovely view of the gas cylinders near Chelsea Harbour.

When the hotel opened in May, the Village newspaper said, 'it marked the realisation of a 16-year battle to turn the 12-acre site into a full service sports and leisure complex. More than 300 guests were at the reception to toast the success of the £53m development, which also includes 46 apartments and penthouses and two new stadium stands.'

Add to that the posh Arkles Restaurant where you can dine on dishes such as tornado of Irish salmon on a fennel and tomato compote, the Shed Bar, adorned with pictures of Ted Drake and Roy Bentley celebrating the championship in 1955, alongside more modern images of Gullit, Bobby Tambling, Peter Bonetti and David Webb, then you are beginning to get an idea of the scale of the thing. It now costs £2,500 to sponsor the match ball.

There is Fishnets, too, where a plate of fish and chips costs £12.50 and inside the hotel, there is the elegant Kings' Brasserie. I have eaten there and I can vouch for it even if the atmosphere could have been improved by a few other diners.

Nor is that the end of it. A new Family Centre was opened in June with a £30,000 indoor play area project that includes a supervised creche. There also will be a Sony Play Station Zone within the centre. The mail order business is thriving to the extent that it has its own warehouse in Camberley, Surrey. To top it all off Chelsea Village also owns Elizabeth Duff Travel, the tenth largest travel agency in the country.

But before you write this off as football gone mad, as a once simple sport sucked ever deeper into the world of Mammon until it has been lost completely from view, remember that one is being run

purely with the object of funding the other. It is progress and Chelsea are benefiting. If they stood still, they would be left behind, they would have no money to attract players of the calibre of Zola and Di Matteo, no stadium worthy of convincing them to come to play in the Premiership.

The old Chelsea is disappearing fast but it is not necessarily being mourned. I walked out of the ground after the win over Vicenza in front of two supporters reminiscing about the bad old days. They were not well-heeled. They were just ordinary fans. They were talking about the days when Chelsea were far from the leading club they are now and when attendances suffered as well. They were laughing about the times the crowd was so sparse they used to be able to run up and down the terraces on The Shed without bumping into anyone else. They could not believe the change that had occurred.

Even if the ground has changed out of all recognition, there are still familiar landmarks in Fulham Road. The Lost Café is still there, where the first-team squad used to go to eat their lunch when there was no canteen at Harlington. Run by a Brazilian from Rio de Janeiro and decked out with pictures of Copacabana Beach and brightly coloured images of pelicans and parrots, it is full to bursting on Saturdays. Alongside the normal café fare such as omelettes and all-day breakfasts, they sell Bahia and Rio sandwiches, traditional Brazilian griddles. Just behind it is Fulham Broadway Methodist Church and it is outside here that one of the matchday bottlenecks occurs. There are hawkers galore at this spot, with their Vialli t-shirts, their scarves and their programme stands. The sellers of the *Chelsea Independent* fanzine stand here, too. They are particularly vociferous in their technique.

Further along towards the stadium, the once unpretentious Indian restaurant that used to be called East India has attempted to capture the spirit of the age by renaming itself Blue Spice. Next to that though, the Sir Oswald Stoll memorial gates, built to honour the dead of the Great War who fell at Arras, Ypres and the Somme, stand unadorned in their dignity.

The march of progress may have cloaked Stamford Bridge itself in glitz and wealth but it has does not appear to have affected the micro-economy on Fulham Road. The stalls have not changed, the burgers appear to be selling just as well. Expensive though they are at £2.50, they are not in the same price range as the £5 take-away fish and chips at Fishnets.

To listen to people such as Chris Manson, the managing director of Chelsea Village Merchandising and Chelsea Village Communications, espousing his own commercial philosophies, is to feel invigorated by the new broom sweeping through English football. Suddenly, the whole thing, all the years of building and construction, of feeling suspicious about what exactly Chelsea Village was and wondering what on earth the effect of it would be on the club, dissolve into misplaced worry.

It seems at last when you look at what is happening at Stamford Bridge that English football supporters are finally being given the sort of arena that American football fans have been enjoying for a long time. The price, just as in the States, is that many supporters can no longer afford to go. It is a heavy cost and a trend that football may come to regret when the bubble bursts, but for now, there is no alternative but to leap on the treadmill. If prices are going up, at least Chelsea are giving their fans something for their high-cost season tickets.

Manson, who used to work for the Really Useful Company co-ordinating Lloyd Webber's forty-nine foreign shows until he got tired of all the travel, has been at the club since the end of 1996. A former season-ticket holder, he trained as an accountant. Now he has become the acceptable, attractive face of football's commercial future.

'I wrote to Ken and said "You need me",' Manson said. 'I had a season ticket but that is not why I am here. I enjoy the football less now. I still enjoy it and I am still fascinated by it but I find I don't enjoy the actual process of watching it so much. It means too much now. It is too tense and I know the characters involved as well so you know a bit too much about what is going on. It is like a stage show, you know, you want to see the show, not what is going on behind.

'I started here looking after special projects, which was all the new developments. Just working for Ken directly. And then that expanded. I recommended that we took the merchandising in house and we changed the way that we did it. We wanted to do it as a high-street store and take the brand up market because the profile of the supporters is much wealthier. You can afford to trade it up and you make much better money over the longer term, having greater profit margins at the higher end rather than Man U's policy of pile it high and sell it cheap.

'I run all the merchandising side and the communications as well. So we are looking at a TV station and a radio station and we are looking to acquire further radio coverage on a proper, permanent basis. At the moment, we have got Radio Chelsea which is just a matchday radio station that broadcasts five miles around the ground but we now broadcast it on the Internet as well.

'When other football clubs have gone on the Net, they have all signed up to Planet on line which delivers a generic service. They deliver a website within a certain framework and you fill in the gaps and everything looks the same. What we have done is a joint venture with IBM so we use their e-commerce. It all

Night falls at the Bridge.

helps to promote the name. By being associated with companies like IBM and Sanyo, it makes us look more professional and more capable. If these people are prepared to deal with us, we are not just a football club and that is what I have been trying to get across.

'We have also bought *Football Monthly* which was a longer-term view. We will lose money on it for the next two to three years but in the longer term the advantages that we have in terms of reach and buying power because of the amount of print we are buying and so on, we can afford to sustain that kind of loss and then emerge at the other end with something which is extremely valuable in three years. But it was important for us to begin to develop business that wasn't necessarily associated with Chelsea FC.

'And in the same way, in the hotel and the restaurant, you will not find any mention of football anywhere apart from in the Shed Bar. It was important for us to do that in other aspects as well. So we bought the tenth biggest travel agency in the UK. They will operate within the group and there are certain cost benefits and marketing benefits in driving people to the hotel and into our restaurants.

'The whole point of the way that the group is structured is that the revenue from all these other sources which will be considerable in their own right will sustain the football club. The football club will not make a profit no matter how much money they make on pay-per-view. There is the hotel and the merchandising and the travel and the restaurants and we are building a 140-bedroom extension to the hotel. Then we have got a joint venture arrangement with the Harbour Club so we will have the Harbour Club down at the far end which will be 80,000 square feet and will be the largest gym in Europe. It will have 4,500 members. That, in turn, will drive people through the restaurants and the hotel and the whole point of that is to sustain the football club. Manson

adds, 'The football business is not a vicious circle but it is a virtual circle in the sense that if you can spend enough to get into the top, you generate so much money that you can afford to stay there. That is how we will get there, with that attitude. A conscious decision was taken a long time before I got here to bring in Hoddle as manager and then Gullit and Vialli and fortunately for us it has worked. People have had a big spending policy in the past and it hasn't worked. But fortunately it has catapulted us from being a West Ham to having a chance of getting up there with Juventus and Barcelona.

'As a football club, we are behind Manchester United in terms of the revenues that we generate. In terms of revenues that are generated from merchandising, the papers always talk about a £30m turnover that Manchester United make but it doesn't actually make that much sense because a lot of that is driven by the wholesale trade which has got a very low margin. So the profit on that is probably only about £3 or £4 million a year. We will be making that in a year's time.

'That will be done partly through the Megastore and partly through direct mail and mail order and partly because we have moved it completely upmarket. The product that we sell in the store is now 75 per cent fashion and 25 per cent football. We are lucky. We have got the name of Chelsea and Kings Road and we have got glamorous, high-profile players and that all makes it relatively fashionable.

'And there will come a point shortly when replica kit will no longer be fashionable to be worn by adults. It will always be worn by kids. For the last three or four years, it has been fashionable to wear the team shirt in the street but that is a relatively new phenomenon. That will stop. That is why we have positioned ourselves in a fashion base. We will get our fingers burnt occasionally but in a very small way

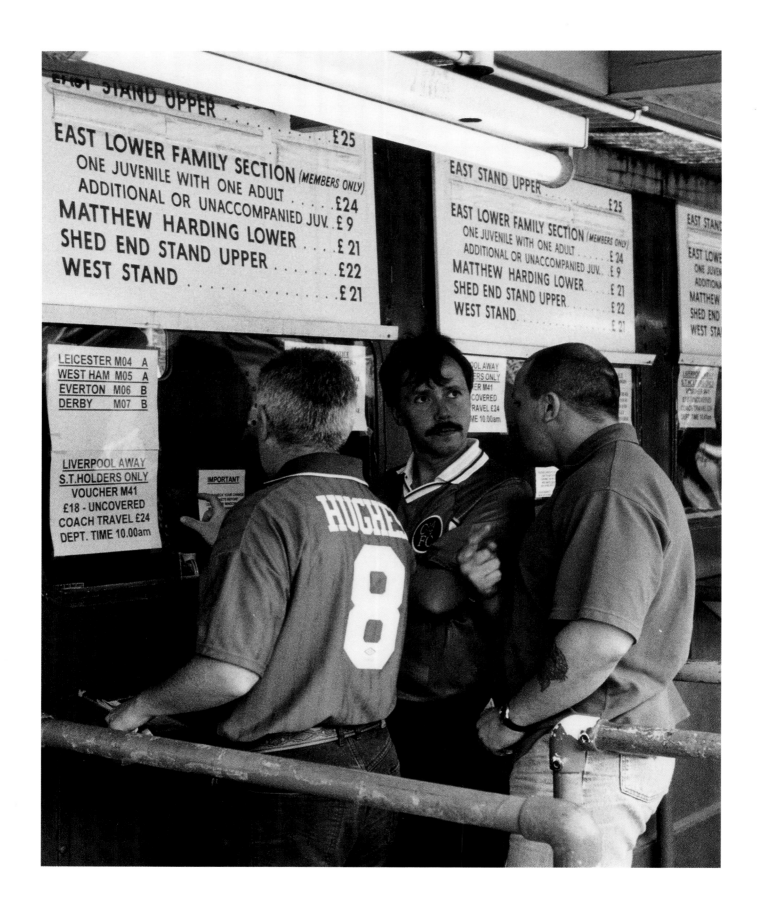

The old ticket stands, another symbol of the past that has now disappeared from Stamford Bridge.

compared to what happens to United or Newcastle. It's like Marks and Spencer. That's what it should be. There is no reason for football merchandise to be crap.

'The quality of the clothing represents something about Chelsea as a whole. If we were to pile it high and sell it cheap it would reflect badly on the four-star hotel that we have got. People would think that the sheets might be slightly dirty or that they would be polyester rather than cotton. Everything that we do has got to reflect those standards.

'We set those standards not because of a snobbish approach to it but because that is who our supporters are, that is our geographical location and that is where the long-term money is. I'm not slagging Man U off but they have a wider base of support but probably a poorer base. They have positioned themselves where they will make the most money out of who they are selling to. We have positioned ourselves to make money out of who we can appeal to given our location and support.

'The Premier League does a survey of 2,000 fans from each club and it shows that the average Chelsea supporter is hugely wealthier than the average football supporter. Wimbledon are ahead of us but the average income for Chelsea is something like £27,000 or £28,000 a year which is a lot bigger than the average for Liverpool or Bolton. We have not done a lot of research of our own up until now because we haven't controlled the merchandising.

Now we control the merchandising and we have built a mail order database of active customers of round about 35,000 in eight months, since we brought the merchandising in house. We can analyse by postcode and we have media response to various different types of activity but the mail order sales that we generate are to rather wider places than the sales that we generate in the Megastore, which is season-

ticket holders, and we can track those through the Loyalty Card. We have basically got the details of about 120,000 or 150,000 but we are going through a process at the moment of bringing all those individual databases together in order to merge them. It is run more like a high-street concern at Chelsea now than at any other football club. They are not souvenir shops any more.

'In Stockholm during the build-up to the Cup Winners Cup, we had four shops and we ran competitions in Swedish to win a weekend in London staying here to watch a game. There is a huge market in Sweden, and more particularly in Norway, and 30 or 40 per cent of the supporters in the stadium on the night of the Cup Winners' Cup were Swedish. We need to make them Chelsea supporters.

'As far as the hotel goes, we have got 60,000 room nights in a year and for next year we have already sold 22,000. It is primarily the business market that we are aiming at. Four hundred yards down that railway track outside the stadium is Earl's Court and another 400 yards further on is Olympia. They are huge conference centres and the market for hotels in this area is severely undersupplied. The time where hotels in London are generally not filled is at weekends but for twenty-eight weekends a year we have got the football on and we are obviously sold out for those because we have sold all the packages to Scandinavian fans.

'In television, Channel Chelsea operates only within the confines of a site on a match day. We want to put ourselves in a position where we have options when the Sky deal runs out in 2001. We will have experience of being able to produce the programming ourselves, we will have a relationship with a cable operator who is able to produce a billing system for pay-per-view. We will just generally know a lot more about the market and have a facility in house

Di Matteo stops Vialli escaping from an interview with Channel Chelsea's Graham Dean about the Italians' club translator, Gary Staker.

Fans pray for a good result as Channel Chelsea broadcasts club news and entertainment around Stamford Bridge.

to be able to produce programming that people want rather than constantly being tied to outside parties who seek to exploit us for their own commercial ends, like Sky.

'We need to put ourselves in a position where we have options. We are trying to open up the market and break out. We are a football club but that does not mean we can't be a rights owner.

'The great model is of the Hollywood Studios. The way they have managed to sell a film into eleven different markets at different times and create the best value for their product is unbelievable. They do it as a cinema release, a secondary release, video release, cable release, satellite release, terrestrial television, that is the kind of thinking football clubs need to get into.

'We provide entertainment and the meaning of life for a huge number of people and other people are exploiting that. All of these fledgling businesses that we are putting together are in order to service the demand, to put ourselves in a position of being the rights owner, to put us in control of our own destiny and we have to do that because it affects the value of everything else that we do. You have to control the way that you are portrayed.'

FOR SOME, PERHAPS, IT MIGHT BE A PARADOX that someone such as Bates, a man whose appearance and public statements mark him out as a traditionalist, is at the head of such a forward-thinking organisation, a club that has become more than a club. But it is he who is driving it forward.

It is no coincidence that in this year that Manson has overseen so many startling advances on the commercial side, so Chelsea have had their most successful season for three decades. 'I am just the tip of the iceberg,' Bates said to me in one of his more modest moments. As Chelsea grows and grows, it seems as if he might be right – even if it is an awfully big tip.

The
Season

WHEN THE FIRST FALL CAME, IT landed on the football world like a great, startling thud. It happened just after 1 p.m. on a Thursday in February. Suddenly, a door was flung open at the training ground at Harlington and Ruud Gullit stormed out, leaving Colin Hutchinson stuck in the middle of trying to tell him he had been sacked. There was a screech of tyres outside and Gullit sped off to Stamford Bridge where his part in the rise of Chelsea was brought to a formal end.

I was driving north on the M6 that morning when I heard the first rumours. Two or three colleagues called me on my mobile phone but they thought it probably was some wildly exaggerated half-truth that had begun to be portrayed as fact. They said that the stories were coming out of Italy, that Italian newspapers were about to run them.

A couple of hours later, the rumours became fact. I was still in the car when another colleague rang to tell me. It was one of those pieces of news that seems so momentous you will always remember where you were when you heard it. Within a few minutes, it was the main headline on Radio Five Live.

If the retirement of Eric Cantona was the biggest football story of 1996/97, this was its equivalent for the 1997/98 season. Perhaps the slow, tortuous slump of Newcastle United and Arsenal's record-breaking championship Double-winning rally ran it close but for the dramatic value of one event that no one was expecting, there was nothing to touch it. When I spoke to *The Times*, I could sense the excitement in the office. In our case, that excitement was tinged with regret: the deputy sports editor is a committed Chelsea supporter.

The second fall of Gullit, the event that drew a line under his love affair with the English game, came two months later. It hardly caused a ripple of publicity in comparison with the sacking but it created an impression on me because I witnessed it at first hand and I felt the sadness in the banality of the events that unfolded.

It happened at Harrods where Gullit was doing the first of a series of book signings to promote his autobiography. The Books Department was crowded with ranks of photographers and film crews about half an hour before Gullit was due to arrive. Along another side of the room, a queue of admirers clutching their copies of his life story snaked out into the Silverware Department.

After a while, when the congestion increased, the female assistants behind the counter started tut-tutting to each other about the disruption the event was causing. The security guards got nervous too and became over-officious in the way that security guards do, trying to clear a path so that customers could fight their way to the luxury toilets and pay their £1 admission.

A few minutes later, Michael Duberry appeared, looking curious. He had stumbled on it all by chance, out shopping with his girlfriend. He came over and asked when Gullit was due. 'I might pop up later for a quick word when things have quietened down,' he said. 'I hope he still remembers who I am.'

It was just after 2 p.m. when Gullit arrived. He looked as dapper as usual and the cameras still sought him out, still loved him. The flashbulbs lit up his face and the photographers yelled for him to look this way and that. For a while, he managed to smile.

Somehow, though, he was different. He did not seem to be drinking in the attention as he used to. The cameras seemed to pierce him, not embrace him, and soon a crease of mild irritation spread across the broad features of his face. The handlers from the

Dutch fans make a pilgrimage to Harlington for autographs from their hero Ruud Gullit.

An inflatable Gullit adorns a supporter's desk at *GQ* magazine.

At Stamford Bridge Gullit wigs became all the rage.

Harrods press office sensed it and brought the photography session to a swift close.

Next, there were the signings. A giant stack of copies of his autobiography sat in front of him on the desk, almost obscuring him from view and his agent, Jon Smith, had anticipated he would be autographing them for two hours. In the end, the line dwindled much quicker than they might have hoped.

Everyone who was there looked delighted to have their books signed, of course, and some muttered words of apology for what had happened as they shoved a Chelsea shirt or programme across the desk for him to sign, too. He was as gracious as always and accepted their good wishes with kind words of his own and a warm smile.

There was something poignant about the whole occasion, though, something sad about this man who had been stripped of some of his dignity and bearing by his sacking and now trying somehow to rediscover it, not embedded in the sport at which he excelled but in a round of publicity-seeking appearances of which this was the first.

Even he seemed unconvinced by it all, trotting his answers out almost by rote, robbed of some of the spontaneity that had made him such a winningly charismatic figure. His smile seemed artificial, thinner than before. His confidence, one of the other things that had given him such allure, had been dented, too, and he spent his time trying to defend himself.

When the queue had petered out, his handlers led Gullit to a small staff room by Etymology and Etiquette where he did a few quick television interviews for English and Italian news stations and then answered a few questions for the English written press.

He admitted he had been stung by suggestions made by Ken Bates in the Chelsea programme the weekend before that he had approached the job as 'a part-time playboy manager'. But instead of leaving the mud-slinging to the chairman and refusing to let himself get dragged into another war of words, he retorted by saying that all the success Chelsea had had since his departure, the Coca-Cola Cup Final victory and the bravura performances in the European Cup Winners' Cup had been down to him.

He said that Vialli had tried to change the style of play and end the rotation system when he took over but that it had not worked so he had gone back to it. He ended by saying that we, the gentlemen of the press, should write what we think, not just report what he and Bates said about each other. Well, here goes: on that day at Harrods, Gullit looked like a man who knew he had lost the war but was still trying to fight the battle.

WHEN THE SEASON HAD BEGUN BACK ON 3 August with Chelsea's appearance in the Charity Shield against the then league champions, Manchester United, there was no hint of an acrimonious end to the Stamford Bridge career of a man who had become synonymous with Chelsea chic ,and had been one of the major influences in turning football supporting from a pursuit of pariahs into one of the favourite hobbies of the chattering classes.

Suddenly, partly because of the cosmopolitan glamour that Gullit bought to the Premiership, partly because of outside influences such as the improvements to stadia forced by the Taylor Report that had been commissioned in the wake of the Hillsborough disaster of 1989, football had become fashionable again, something that bestowed a certain laddish trendiness on anyone who followed it.

Gullit was very much in the vanguard of the revolution. In the autumn of 1997, his dreadlocked image seemed to be everywhere, staring out from the

The ever-present pressmen
surround Zola before a
game, hoping for a story.

The gentlemen of the
press quiz Gullit upstairs
at Harlington.

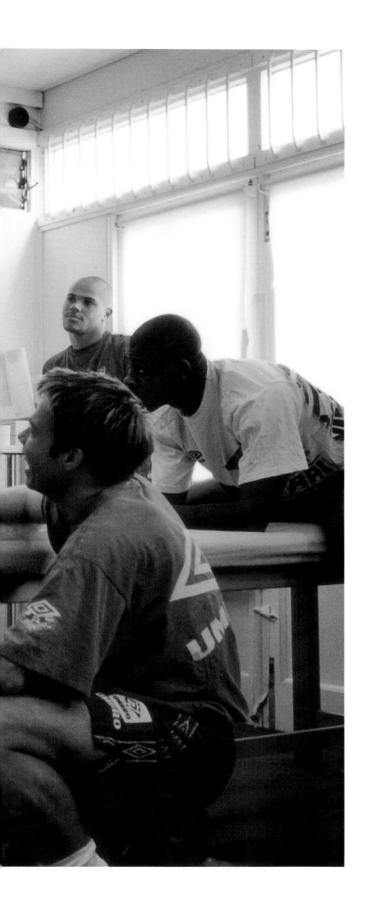

Gullit holds court regaling Tore Andre Flo,
Andy Myers, Eddie Newton and Graham Le Saux with
anecdotes of Marco Van Basten.

Graham Le Saux reads the papers with his wife in their Kensington home.

Gullit brought Le Saux back to Chelsea from Blackburn.

sides of London buses advertising his own clothes range, on the cover of the Virgin magazine that stocked every rack in every carriage on every train shuttling between London and Liverpool or Manchester. His smiling face was plastered on the windows of every Pizza Hut outlet across the country, too, and on every table of each of its restaurants. In newsagents, it would be a rarity if he was not the cover story on at least one of the style magazines and the football glossies. He was ubiquitous.

He seemed to have spent wisely, too, as he built the team in the wake of their FA Cup victory the previous May. Before last season began, he bought the Dutch goalkeeper, Ed De Goey, from Feyenoord, the Uruguayan midfielder, Gustavo Poyet, from Real Zaragoza, the Nigerian defender, Celestine Babayaro, from Anderlecht, the French midfielder, Bernard Lambourde, from Bordeaux, and the Norwegian forward, Tore Andre Flo, from SK Brann Bergen. Then, on the eve of the new season, he topped them all by smashing Chelsea's transfer record and paying £5m to bring the England wing back, Graeme Le Saux, back to Stamford Bridge. The negotiations between Le Saux and Colin Hutchinson had gone on through the night but Ruud had got his man and he was paraded proudly at Harlington on the Friday morning before the first round of matches began.

Manchester United were the clear favourites to retain their title but there were many other observers, Alex Ferguson, the United manager, among them, who considered Chelsea to be the main threat to their hegemony, quite clearly the growing force in the Premiership.

Things did not start particularly well. After losing the Charity Shield in a penalty shoot-out, Gullit and his team lost the first league match of the season away at unfancied Coventry City, too. Then they recovered by thrashing the new boys, Barnsley, 6–0,

a performance that included four beautifully-taken goals by Vialli.

By the beginning of November, they had moved up to fourth place despite defeats to Arsenal and Liverpool and, after a chaotic first leg in the snow and ice of the Arctic Circle, they had overcome the Norwegian part-timers, Tromso, with a 7–1 victory in west London to progress to the third round of the European Cup Winners' Cup.

By the end of November, they had moved up to second place with a 4–0 home win over Derby County but still there was an uneasy feeling that everything was not quite right, that somehow all the success they were enjoying was dreadfully brittle, ready to crack at any moment. Even in those heady times near the top of the table, there was tension in the air.

Some of it was to do with the rotation system that Gullit insisted on operating and that became a fixation for the media. From week to week and match to match, it was impossible to predict the team that Gullit would pick, so fickle and apparently without rationale were his choices. Gullit denied it but to most it seemed as though his chopping and changing was preventing players finding their rhythm. He said it was the new way of European football, that there were so many demands on players that a squad system was essential. The players kept their counsel but they were disquieted. The week after Vialli scored four at Barnsley, for instance, he was dropped for the home match against Southampton. In December, Flo scored a hat-trick against Tottenham Hotspur and then had to make way for Vialli a fortnight later. Gullit said it again: it was just the way the modern game was, that he needed to use a squad system to keep his players fresh for the avalanche of games that rushed at them, that football was not just about eleven players any more.

'In some ways, it can be difficult to cope with,' Mark Hughes said as he sat at one of the canteen tables that winter. 'Strikers more than anyone like to get into a rhythm and they thrive on the confidence that comes with regular games. You can't get that at the moment. But I'm not really complaining about it. The thing that makes it acceptable to the players, I think, is that it is changed so often that if you are not in the team one week, you know you have got a very good chance of being in it the next week.'

But still there was this creeping unease. It got worse at the beginning of January when Chelsea opened their defence of the FA Cup against Manchester United at Stamford Bridge. United were in rampant form at the time, so far ahead in the championship that it seemed inconceivable that anyone could catch them, so bursting with confidence and verve were they. But they were the measuring stick against which ambitious clubs like Chelsea had to set themselves.

The game was a disaster. United were brilliant and Chelsea were overrun. Almost before they knew it, the unthinkable had happened and they were 5–0 down. They saved a little pride with three late goals, including a sublime chip from Le Saux, but the message had been boomed over loud and clear: they were still an age away from achieving the kind of quality and fluency that United had. The result was a severe shock to the Chelsea system and up in his seat in the front row of the directors' box, Ken Bates furrowed his brow.

It was about then that the whispers started that Gullit was not treating his duties with the respect they deserved.

More significantly, there was also a sort of revisionist movement beginning, a new anti-Gullit feeling that somehow seemed to be a precursor of the bubble bursting. Robert Crampton started it

in *The Times* Saturday magazine with a damning portrait of a rude, self-obsessed and not particularly articulate man who was in the midst of an orgy of narcissism. Much later, Sally Weale in the *Guardian* mocked his intellect.

Gradually, it seemed that the spell was wearing off, that people had stopped being dazzled by his charm and his dynamism. The supporters did not feel it. They were to remain loyal to the end but elsewhere, in the minds of the people who mattered, this shift, this change in the mood was noted. Gullit never really seemed to recover from the ignominy of that defeat to United. It was as if the game had exposed him, albeit briefly, as a charlatan of a coach and the taste never went away. At the same time, off the field, Hutchinson and Bates, mindful of the fact that they had been left in the lurch two seasons earlier when Glenn Hoddle had deserted them for the England manager's job, were growing restless because Gullit was stalling on signing a new contract.

It was infuriating enough for journalists trying to pin him down about the negotiations. He was the very soul of assurance, of course, shrugging his shoulders nonchalantly, saying that the time would come when he would sit down and talk with Bates and he was sure that everything would be agreed but they did not need to do it yet. In private, it appears he felt the same way. It never occurred to him that the club might call his bluff.

Part of the nub of the problem, part of the reason for this almost intangible feeling of tension that was drifting through the club from top to bottom, and which Gullit appeared not to understand, was that his refusal to negotiate was having debilitating knock-on effects. It was creating uncertainty lower down the scale. It was here, perhaps, that his ego became his Achilles heel.

He did not realise, or appear to care, that his

Dan Petrescu heads off the line in the FA Cup match against United, who won 5–3 to put the holders out.

Gullit shows his frustration from the touchline. The control was ebbing away.

Gullit faces the media after a poor midweek
league game.

Gianluca Vialli chats with Graham Rix at Harlington. Their relationship was close even before Vialli's promotion.

refusal to sign was blocking any offer of new long-term contracts to men who might be vulnerable if he left and a new manager wanted to bring in staff of his own. Men such as Gwyn Williams and Graham Rix, the physios and the reserve and youth-team managers were all facing uncertain futures and it had begun to affect the atmosphere at Harlington. About that time, the players even staged their own behind-closed-doors crisis meeting. It was a sign that matters were reaching a climax.

Even though the thought of the club sacking him still would have been greeted with general contempt and disbelief, the unrest increased at the end of January when Gullit made a rare starting appearance in the Coca-Cola Cup semi-final first leg against Arsenal at Highbury. He looked a sad shadow of the player who had been considered the best in Europe. Playing at sweeper, he seemed out of shape and out of his depth. He was directly to blame for one of the two Arsenal goals that seemed to have ended Chelsea's interest in the competition even though Mark Hughes, a second-half substitute, gave them hope by pulling one goal back.

He did not know it then, of course, but another defeat at Highbury on Sunday 8 February, was his last league game in charge. The following Tuesday, he played for the reserves against Queens Park Rangers reserves. It was a 0–0 draw. It was his last game for Chelsea. Two days later, with Chelsea second in the Premiership, Colin Hutchinson made his visit to Harlington.

Events moved bewilderingly quickly. After Gullit had left Hutchinson in mid-sentence at the training ground, he phoned ahead to say he wanted to see Bates at Stamford Bridge and set off along the M4 into west London. He had been told by Hutchinson that the board of directors had found his financial demands unacceptable and had decided to look for a new coach. Astonished, he wanted clarification from the chairman.

Gullit, still thinking at that stage that he would continue as coach until the end of the season, spoke to his agent, Jon Smith, on his mobile phone and discovered he had been told by a journalist that Gullit appeared on the verge of being replaced. Suddenly, he began to understand that he might be in the process of being sacked.

By now, Gullit had been told that Bates was in Drakes, one of the eateries at Stamford Bridge and because of a tight schedule he might not be able to meet him. Gullit drove to the stadium anyway and parked outside. Eventually, he was told to meet Bates at the Conrad Hotel in Chelsea Harbour at 4.30 pm. He called Smith again and Smith told him that the news of his sacking had now appeared on Teletext.

Gullit drove to his apartment in Cadogan Square and began to suspect that he had been the victim of a plot. His suspicions centred on the manoeuvrings of a deal he had been trying to complete for the Glasgow Rangers winger, Brian Laudrup. Laudrup had cancelled a planned meeting on the pretext that his wife was ill but Gullit found out that the previous week, he had visited London, been picked up at the airport by Gwyn Williams and taken to lunch with Vialli and Gianfranco Zola.

After Chelsea had held a press conference at Drakes announcing Vialli as the new manager, Gullit finally got his meeting with Bates at the Conrad Hotel at 6.30 pm. Bates said the decision had been Hutchinson's. Before Gullit left, Bates handed him a letter. He read it when he got to his car. He was sacked and he was no longer even allowed access to the training ground.

Taken totally by surprise, Gullit, Smith and his First Artist Corporation were utterly outflanked by Chelsea's masterful public relations operation. By releasing details of Gullit's wage demands, they had smeared him with the pungent liquid of greed. Hutchinson said Gullit's opening gambit had been an annual salary of £2m a year net which would have cost the club £3.2m. Soon, Gullit's demand that the figure he was asking be 'netto' not gross had become a popular catchphrase, almost a byword for avarice. By hiring Vialli, a fans' favourite, Chelsea had managed to deflect the opprobrium that would have been unleashed upon them with the firing of Gullit.

The next day, Friday the 13th, after Smith had rung round all the national newspapers rubbishing Chelsea's claims, Gullit tried to wrest the initiative back and a press conference was held for him at The International Sportsman's Club beneath Barkers department store in Kensington High Street. It was a rather grand name for a basement bar that, in its previous incarnation as Scribes West, had been the personal karaoke bar of Terry Venables.

It was an unsuitably small venue. By the time Gullit arrived, it was mobbed, heaving with hundreds of reporters and tens of film crews all trying to crowd into the room where the deposed manager was led to a small table in the corner. In a bar to one side, those of us who did not have the stomach for the fight, or the skill to shoe-horn ourselves into a position of proximity to Gullit, watched proceedings on a big screen that had been set up specially for the occasion.

It was sad to see Gullit sit there. This man who had once been so proud and so cocky looked stunned. His spirit seemed shattered. He said he had been up all night. For the first time, he was actually showing transparently that something mattered to him. He had departed from the casual air of insouciance that characterised everything else he had talked about in his Chelsea career until then.

He talked now of a conspiracy and said how disappointed he was in his staff. He also made one fairly clumsy attempt to mobilise the support of the Chelsea hardcore by invoking the memory of Matthew Harding and saying that this would never have happened if he had been alive.

At one stage, he even appeared to be wiping away a tear as the cameras rolled. Later, though, he moved into another, smaller room to talk to the written press. In there, he was close to being back to his old self, cocky and jokey. He said he had not been made any financial offer by the club and that as far as he was concerned, negotiations had only just begun. His demand for £2m might have been high but he had always intended that there be room for compromise. That Chelsea showed no inclination to deal only increased his suspicions of a plot.

Throughout, the most striking thing about the press conference, apart from Gullit's subdued demeanour, was that he spoke as though he was sitting in the witness box at a trial. As he relayed the tale of the machinations over Laudrup, he repeatedly referred to Zola as 'Mr Franco Zola' and Vialli as 'Mr Luca Vialli'.

He told the story about Laudrup not being able to make the journey south to see him because his wife was ill. 'I thought why doesn't he just come by himself?' Gullit said. 'Then, when I found out they had lunch, I realised that everything had already been planned behind my back.'

He carried on from there, hitting his stride. 'I think I gave this club a lot,' he said. 'I gave them success that no one could have dreamt we would have achieved. Now I just want to know what the real reason is for me getting the sack. The money is only a stick they tried to hit me with. Even the man on the street knows that this is not the real reason.

'If they had made me an offer, I would have stayed because I wanted to stay at Chelsea. What has happened will be a question mark for the rest of my life but they can never take away from me what I achieved at Chelsea. I am still a little bit confused by it all. I am used to coaches being sacked because they are at the bottom but now one has been sacked because he has done so well. I had a very good time at Chelsea and I had some great plans for the club. To win the championship and maybe even something more. I am sad because I can no longer finish this.'

Soon, though, it became apparent that, even if a modest amount of forward planning had gone on, it was less a conspiracy than a growing realisation on the parts of Bates and Hutchinson that they and Gullit had certain mutually incompatible intentions about the future of the player-manager. Some claimed that Ken Bates resented the profile that Gullit had assumed. Gullit himself, while refusing to state this publicly, has suggested as much in hints and quasi-allegations.

Bates, though, has flatly denied this and even if there was an element of envy, he is too astute a businessman to jettison somebody just because they are popular. Instead, it appears he and Hutchinson had gradually become convinced that Gullit had achieved as much as he could at Chelsea and that rather than engage in debilitating and pointless negotiating, they ought to make a quick, clean break.

Central to this thinking was the fact that Gullit, under financial pressure because of obligations to his estranged wife, Christina, was seeking a salary based on his continuance as a player and a manager whereas Chelsea wanted him to concentrate on managing. They did not believe he was committed enough to his job to be able to do both and they judged that his fitness had suffered as a result. Gullit, though, was insistent that no one but he would dictate when the end of his playing career would come.

If Gullit had secured anywhere near the salary he was demanding, it would have made him by far the highest-paid manager in England with wages that outstripped those earned by Alex Ferguson and Kenny Dalglish, men who had proven their ability by winning trophy after trophy. Chelsea were not prepared to go to those lengths to keep him, and rather than drag out the whole affair they instead acted swiftly and decisively.

On the Chelsea clubcall line, the Tuesday after Gullit's sacking, Bates spoke at length about this side of the club's dissatisfaction with Gullit. 'We did not want a player-coach who was not playing,' Bates said. 'Since Ruud took over, we played 84 games. He started 10 and was sub in 14. His job was to run the playing side and not to sell pizzas. But towards the end, he had a very aggressive commercial manager lining him up all sorts of jobs.

'What with that and him trying to get his Dutch coaching badge, we had to ask what his priorities were. We felt there weren't enough hours in the day for him to train as a player, run the club and carry out his extensive commercial activities. It was reasonable to ask him to give up playing but Ruud said that wasn't a decision for us to make. I agreed with that but it was for Chelsea to decide whether we wanted to pay him as a player. And at £3.75m a year, we didn't. With the squad we have we should be in the FA Cup instead of Manchester United, maybe five points ahead of them instead of behind in the league, and I'm not too happy we're a goal down against Arsenal either.'

The players and the coaching staff were caught up in the middle of the turmoil. Some, such as Frank Leboeuf, who had been at Gullit's flat on the day he was sacked, were worried lest their loyalty to the former player-manager be construed as disloyalty to his successor. Suddenly, it became clear that far more

The player–manager: Gullit leaves the pitch after
a rare, and disappointing, appearance.

than just the futures of Gullit and Vialli were at stake. For once, the footballers at Chelsea could share something with working men everywhere: when a new boss takes over, you fear for your job.

Graeme Le Saux spoke for most of the players when he said how stunned he had been by the turn of events. 'I can't tell you how much of a shock it was,' he said. 'In a funny sense, you keep expecting him to come back – as if he's just gone away for a week. You try to work out why it all happened, if it's all for the best, and look at the politics of it all. But as a player, you have to be professional. I spoke to a couple of the others and we decided that whatever happens no one must let it be an excuse for under-achieving.'

The players knew nothing of what was going on until Thursday afternoon. They had had a normal training session with Gullit in the morning and had been largely unaware of his fateful meeting with Hutchinson. Le Saux learned of the first rumours through a phone call from his agent, Jon Holmes. Later, his wife, Marianne, rang him to tell him that the news was on Ceefax. Some of them discussed what had happened, either on the telephone that night or standing round in informal groups at Harlington. There was an air of faint disbelief but there was no anger.

This was an object lesson in how easy it can be to effect a coup like that in a football club, with even a modicum of planning. The players may have been momentarily disoriented by the change but they knew they had the Coca-Cola Cup semi-final second leg with Arsenal, one of the biggest matches of their season, fast approaching and that the club had to pull together if it had a chance of reaching Wembley.

For some reason, perhaps because they are essentially a group of individuals brought up on win bonuses and the culture of life going on whatever happens at management level, there never seems to be any real threat of the equivalent of industrial action, even when a popular boss is fired. Football may be an industry now and footballers may have a union but for people who can be assertive in other areas, they seem remarkably compliant in the fact that they have no say whatsoever in who it is they work for.

Unless they act together – and there is now little chance of that in a world that has become so material and image-conscious – there would be no chance of making a stand for a manager. Realistically, popular though Gullit had been with many of his players, they did not have the inclination to make an issue of his departure anyway. Many of them rang him to sympathise, but at Harlington, it was simply business as usual.

Others, though, were actively relieved about his departure. Latterly, Graham Rix, starved of responsibility, had not been enjoying himself under Gullit. He had lost some of his motivation, some of the spark and the life that have made him one of the most highly rated coaches in the country. When Gullit was deposed, Rix spoke out against him in an article in the *News of the World* and some labelled him a traitor, one of the conspirators that Gullit had refused to identify.

In the article, under the headline 'I Saw Gullit Crack Up', Rix spoke first about Gullit's antics at half-time in the league defeat against Arsenal and portrayed a man who was on the verge of buckling under the pressure of managing one of the top teams in the Premiership.

'It was half-time, we were 2–0 down and Rudi was on his own in the showers,' Rix said. 'I walked in and he was hitting his fist against his forehead over and over again. In his other hand, he had a piece of paper with the team he wanted for the second half.

I looked at it and there were only two defenders. I couldn't believe it. I told him "You can't do that, there's no backbone to the team". And I quickly scribbled out what I thought the team should be. I told him I was going to leave him alone for thirty seconds to get himself together. When I came back, he had written up my team and was ready to tell the players about the changes.

'It was clear to me things weren't going as well as his cool exterior suggested. The guy was really struggling. I was desperate for him to ask me for help. But he never asked. It was heart-breaking. I worked with Ruud for eighteen months and I can honestly say I never knew the guy. I think deep down Rudi is quite insecure and the cool thing is just a front. What has happened now is probably for the best because we have gone badly off the rails in recent weeks. I'm not sure Ruud could have halted the slide.

'There were many times when I had to tell him 'You can't do this'. At Leeds last season, we were 2–0 down after just nine minutes and he told three of the subs to warm up. I asked him what he was doing and he said he was making two substitutions. I couldn't believe it. I said "You can't do that, you can't take two players off after only nine minutes, you will destroy them." But he would not listen. He was adamant. So I said "You will make yourself look stupid. You are admitting you have made an almighty mistake." He listened to that. And he decided he wasn't going to make the substitutions after all.

'But Rudi would never confide in me. Sometimes we would work on something all week in training and on Saturday he'd change his mind. Ruud never confided in me or anyone. It was as if he only trusted himself. I was his coach and I had to back him up. When players came to me complaining I told them Ruud was the boss. I always stood by him. That's not to say I didn't put over my point of view in private.

'He did have outstanding successes. There was the time we were 2–0 down at home to Liverpool and on our way out of the FA Cup. Rudi wanted to make changes but I was against it. Liverpool were on fire and I wanted to keep it as it was and try to keep the score down. But Rudi put Mark Hughes on and played with three up front and we turned it round and won 4–2. It was a real masterstroke. That was probably his greatest moment but it also became a problem. Having succeeded with drastic measures once, Rudi felt it would work every time.

'After I had got over the shock of the news, I went down to see Luca in the dressing room. He was very happy, with a big grin on his face. I was pleased when he said he wanted me to stay on. He is a lovely guy, so honest. I wished him all the best and his first words to me were "Graham, I need your help". It was amazing. I had waited eighteen months for Rudi to say that.'

The following Wednesday, the day of Chelsea's Coca-Cola Cup semi-final second leg against Arsenal, the *Chelsea Independent* fanzine carried a picture of Rix next to Gullit on the grass at a training session. Gullit is saying 'There is no reason we cannot become the biggest club in the world' and Rix is replying 'I can think of two million reasons.' The headline above this scene was 'Et Tu Rixy? Did Graham knife Ruud?' Once more, though, the conspiracy theorists were disappointed when it came to the role of Rix. He had felt a change was needed and he has made no attempt to deny that but he was shocked that events had moved as quickly as they did. Even a few weeks before the end of the season, he still spoke vividly of the shock he felt when he was told the news.

'I got a bit of stick after Rudi went,' Rix said, 'people saying that I stabbed him in the back. But I had absolutely no idea about it. I swear on my little

The atmosphere of the Chelsea dugout grew tense as the relationship between Gullit and Rix degenerated.

boy's life. He was released or relieved of his duties on the Thursday at about ten past one at the training ground. I didn't know until about 1.30. Colin Hutchinson called me in and said "Sit down Rico, Rudi's no longer in charge". I said "You what?". He said: "He's no longer in charge and Luca's taking over". So it was one hammer blow after another. But he said "Luca does want to keep the same staff".

'Rudi keeps saying there was a hidden agenda and all that sort of thing but I think it's a bit unfair. I actually tried to phone him that day and for whatever reason I couldn't get hold of him. I eventually got hold of him the next day and he was quite aggressive and said he was disappointed. And I said "Well don't be disappointed with me because I have done nothing wrong".

'I think there needed to be a change. The thing that was disappointing me was not the way he was going about his job. It disappointed me the fact that there were good people at the club who were not earning a great deal of money who needed to be looked after: the youth coach, the physios, the reserve coach, the goalkeeper coach, myself, Gwyn. We weren't earning big money but we had been a good staff and we needed to be looked after. The club had to look at it from their point of view. There was no way they were going to give out three-year or four-year deals to all those people if Rudi wasn't going to sign. I just thought that as a manager, one of his responsibilities was surely to look after the staff, and I don't think he did as well as he could in that particular respect.'

BEHIND THE SCENES, THEN, behind that facade of bonhomie, behind the supposition that Chelsea under Gullit was the happiest of ships, the manager had made himself all sorts of powerful enemies.

His only mistake, he thought, was being too trusting, not a quality one would readily associate with one so canny as Gullit, with someone who was linked with a return to English football with Fulham and Tottenham Hotspur within weeks of his departure from Chelsea. 'I owe a lot to the English game although I have had bad experiences,' he said. 'People behave badly. But I have noticed that if a bad thing happens, you settle down and think about it, maybe you get a bit older, more mature and you realise that on both sides, a whole lot of things could have been avoided. You know, maybe if you had thought more about the human part and not only about the business part.'

If that was as close to regrets as Gullit got, Bates had none. At that Drakes press conference where the appointment of Vialli was announced, Bates took centre stage. 'Life goes on,' he said. 'The king is dead. Long live the king.'

I T WAS EASY to understand the rationale. One superstar is shown the door, another walks in. One big name, one figurehead to attract the best of the world's players, is told to leave, another is clasped to the Chelsea bosom. At first, it seemed Chelsea and their fans were getting like for like when Gianluca Vialli took over from Ruud Gullit on that traumatic February Thursday, that the join was almost seamless. The reality was very different.

Vialli, like Gullit, was a footballing icon, that much is true. I remembered him from his days at the Genoese club, Sampdoria, when he still had a mop of frizzy hair and he and Roberto Mancini led their team to a European Cup Final against Barcelona at Wembley, a match lost to a spearing free-kick from Ronald Koeman that took the trophy to Catalonia instead of Italy.

He was the son of a millionaire and had started his career with Cremonese before the move to Samp, when he and Mancini inspired their Serie A championship victory in 1991. Vialli was the league's leading scorer with sixteen goals.

During a subsequent spell at Juventus, he strengthened his reputation as one of Italy's leading strikers and one of their best-known personalities. He played in attack there, after they paid Sampdoria what was then a world record fee of £12.5m for him. He partnered Fabrizio Ravanelli, the White Feather who later brought Middlesbrough so much anguish and frustration, and this time they won the European Cup in 1996, with Vialli as their captain. He had won fifty-nine caps for Italy.

But still we had no idea what he was really like. He had a torrid time when he moved to Chelsea. In his first season, Gullit would not play him, not regularly at least. Some said it was because Gullit was jealous, because the Megastore was selling more posters of Vialli than it was of the player-coach. Gullit just laughed that off. Mostly, people thought that maybe it was because Vialli was over the hill. He smoked, it was said. There were hints of a dissolute London lifestyle.

There were suggestions, too, of a rift between him and the manager who had brought him to London from Turin. Vialli must have found it difficult to go from the acclaim of having been at the pinnacle of his profession as he lifted the European Cup to being a bit-part player in an ambitious Premiership side. He confided his frustrations in private to some of his friends in the Italian press but in public he kept a dignified silence.

In his second year, he came back for the start of the new season having worked harder than ever to get into shape. He had quit smoking and the results seemed to show. In the second game of the Premiership season, away at Barnsley, he scored four clinically taken goals, the best a run and first-time shot after a beautifully curled pass into his path from Dan Petrescu. Chelsea won 6–0.

There were other highlights before the turn of the year, notably the two goals he scored to save Chelsea's blushes in the Arctic Circle when they were in danger of being humiliated in the snow by the Norwegian part-timers of Tromso. In the return leg, which Chelsea won 7–1, Vialli rounded things off with a hat-trick. He was still a hero with the Stamford Bridge supporters.

But it was really only when the regicide was over, when Gullit had been removed and Vialli installed, that his personality was brought into the public view. Suddenly, we discovered a quietly-spoken, modest, gentle-seeming man who appeared to be as far away from a playboy as it was possible to be.

At first, there was a widespread feeling of shock that Bates and Hutchinson had chosen a man who

had no experience of management, especially as they seemed to be so unhappy with the player-manager role that Gullit had refused to relinquish. In some quarters, Vialli was seen as a panic measure, a stop-gap until someone more established, such as Terry Venables, could be appointed. When one newspaper suggested that scenario was to take place, a writ winged its way out of Chelsea Village to the author. Soon, it became known that Hutchinson had made a sort of managerial scouting trip to Turin to sound out some of the Juventus directors and personnel, to gauge their opinion on what sort of a manager Vialli would make. Hutchinson returned to London with words of praise ringing in his ears. In Turin, they had nothing but respect for Luca.

Perhaps the most glowing testament had come from the man whose opinion everyone respected most. Marcello Lippi, the coach who guided Juventus to four successive European finals, who has continued to succeed even when his star strikers have been sold out from under him, who has been such a profound influence on Alex Ferguson, the Manchester United manager, and his assistant, Brian Kidd, could not say enough about his former striker and the challenge of management.

'On this occasion there was only one route open to him and that was to enjoy the honour of becoming Chelsea's manager,' Lippi said. 'There is only one thing you need to know about Luca and that is he was born to leadership just as a baby is born to his mother's breast. He will take to management as naturally as a baby suckles from its mother.

'People who know him well know that he has a pedigree and the bigger the challenge, the more he rises to it. Throughout his playing career, it was the same whether it was for a club or the national team and never once did he attempt to hide from any task. It will be the same as a manager.'

But now we began to discover this man that Lippi was talking about. For those of us who had not known him, who had never really come across him at the occasional player press conferences he had been asked to participate in at Harlington, it was like a revelation. Where Gullit's ego had been over-powering, his sense of self overwhelming, Vialli displayed a refreshing humility. If Vialli had hidden behind an apparently loose command of English, he came before us now as a thoroughly articulate speaker, someone whose use of idiom and metaphor was far more advanced than Gullit's. Where Gullit had finished his sentences with extravagant gestures that were great for television but rarely translated into print, Vialli was an emotive speaker who talked with passion and intelligence.

If his future had been uncertain because of the way Gullit had treated him, an imminent move to management had not crossed his mind. At the age of thirty-three, he still had perhaps a couple more years of playing at the top level left in him, probably away from Chelsea, back in Italy. Then Bates and Hutchinson threw him in at the deep end and left him to sink or swim. Those who knew him never had any doubt which option he would take.

Vialli did not make any rash promises, any startling predictions, when he took over. It soon became apparent he was not that type of player-manager. The word spread quickly that he was more of a listener than Gullit had been, that he did not interpret taking advice from others as a sign of weakness. He wanted to watch, to be involved at all levels of the club. On his first Monday in charge, he even went to watch the reserves at Kingstonian, something Gullit had not done for an age. At his first press conference, the hastily-arranged affair in Drakes that was stage-managed by Bates, Vialli sat next to Gary Staker, the interpreter he did not really need, and addressed the hordes of media as a player-manager for the first time. He spoke immediately about honesty and understanding, about how he wanted the players to trust him. 'I want to improve the relationships between management and players,' he said. 'I think an honest rapport is the key to any successful team. I would like to make the players more animated and increase enthusiasm, to let players know why I make decisions, so they know why I am doing something rather than something else.'

Some of this was aimed at Gullit. Many of the Chelsea team felt puzzled by the way Gullit had treated them. They were angry at the cavalier way he treated their feelings and never saw the need to explain his decisions to them. They did not get any feedback from him. He was a dictator at the training ground, his word was law and that was the end of it.

What Vialli was offering, in the lingua franca of an American presidential election, was a kinder, gentler Chelsea, a Chelsea run almost by the players for the players, certainly with more input from the staff. His was to be a consensual rule and although he said he feared he would have to change, that he would not be able to maintain friendships with those who had once been his teammates because of the need to establish a distance between them, he was eager to earn their respect.

In that area, he had a head start. Always one of the most popular players at the club, both with team-mates and supporters, he had fitted in easily with the boisterous members of the team such as Dennis Wise. At a time when Vialli had been out of the team, Wise had even gone so far as to pull up his club shirt during a match to reveal a message to him on a t-shirt underneath: 'Cheer up Luca, we love you'.

Now, they did not quite know how to treat their new boss. On his first day in charge, he did not get

changed with them at Harlington. Instead of pulling his kit on in the players' rooms to the right of the double doors, he went to the left where the staff got ready, and changed with them. It was a difficult day for him.

The following Monday, he held his first official press conference at Harlington as the player-manager. Two days later, Chelsea were due to face Arsenal, then in the midst of a superlative unbeaten run, in the second leg of their Coca-Cola Cup semi-final. They trailed 2–1 from the first leg and Arsenal were most people's favourites to go through.

By a fluke of unfortunate timing, thirty members of the Dutch airforce trooped into Harlington that Monday morning like an avenging band of Gullit's countrymen. They looked a little sheepish as they stood and watched training from behind the glass of the canteen windows, the victims of an invitation that had gone past its sell-by date.

Before long, though, they had been thoroughly upstaged by Vialli. It was half term and Harlington was crammed full of children in team shirts. Some brought toddlers in push-chairs, others hung around clutching autograph books. The car park was full to overflowing and on the road outside, cars obscured the verge for several hundred yards. Even after the players had walked off the pitches at the end of training, still they came, eager to witness the start of a new era.

Upstairs, there were almost as many members of the media. At the back, camera crews jostled for position on the dais. Gwyn Williams barked out orders, telling them to calm down or they would have to get out. Flashbulbs popped, tape recorders whirred.

Before Vialli came upstairs, Mark Hughes and Wise were brought up to give their reaction to the dramatic events of the past few days, to talk about how they were adapting to such a sudden change

D-Day at Chelsea: Gianluca Vialli flanked by Colin Hutchinson (on his right) translator Gary Staker and Ken Bates (on his left), is paraded in front of the world's media as Gullit's replacement.

Quickly adapting to his new role, Vialli fields questions from representatives of the *Sun*, *Press Association*, *Daily Star*, *Guardian* and other papers.

and life under their new manager. Both gave the impression that they were optimistic about what the future held and about the capabilities of Vialli.

'I was always impressed with the dignity with which he dealt with being out of the side last season,' Hughes said. 'I sit next to him in the dressing room and before every game he would wish me luck and you knew he genuinely meant it. Most of us thought he'd become a coach. He did not mention it but he has a presence. I'm looking forward to working with him. He's passionate about the game and he played in Italy where they have a different attitude, where the emphasis is on stopping teams playing.'

Wise was next. 'He's a wonderful man,' he said, smiling wickedly. 'I like him as a person and I am looking forward to helping him. He still messes about and enjoys a joke with us. We still call him Luca. We liked Ruud, we like Luca. It is the club's decision about what happened to Ruud and the players just have to accept it. They haven't explained it to us but clubs never do.'

Then Vialli came in and the room hushed. There were instructions from Gwyn about when the Italians could ask questions and when it would be the turn of the English. Vialli looked a little nervous. His head was clean shaven. His chin and his cheeks were not. But when he spoke, he seemed to cast his listeners under a spell.

'This is a very difficult and exciting position,' he said. 'I will have to be like a sponge and absorb as much as possible. Before, I was a teammate, a friend. Now I will have to make decisions and upset them. I want to be honest with them, open, blunt if necessary. Players want to know why and I will explain my decisions. They might not understand, they might think I'm wrong, but I want my conscience clear and I hope they will respect my decision.

'The players need to care about you to play well for you. The players are intelligent enough to understand it is a team game, not a game for single minds. If they are dropped, I hope they keep going and try to make me change my mind. I might do if I see the players work very hard in training and have the right spirit. If you are playing, everything is easy, you are happy and confident. When you don't play, you must be mature and help your teammates to perform. If you can do that, you are even better than the top scorer of the club.'

He was asked then about the circumstances in which he had inherited the job and whether he felt guilty about what had happened to Gullit. It was put to him that there had been suggestions he had stabbed his predecessor in the back and that he had been the ringleader of a players' revolt.

'I will start from where Rudi left off,' Vialli said calmly. 'I respond to my own conscience. At the end of the day, you have to look in the mirror and you know if you have done something wrong. It is the way you behave day to day which shows people if you are a backstabber or not. No one stabbed Rudi in the back, not the staff or the players. This decision has come from the board. Even though we were not the best of friends and we had our problems professionally, I wish him all the best.'

When Wednesday came and Arsenal arrived at Stamford Bridge, the excitement was almost at fever pitch. There was a fierce anticipation mixed in with it, too, an apprehension, perhaps, that some of the magic, some of the glamour that Gullit had instilled in Chelsea might have flown back to Holland with him and that Vialli might be exposed as some naive impostor, a placeman to buy time for Bates and Hutchinson.

Between Fulham Broadway tube station and the ground, the street vendors were cashing in on the new appointment. T-shirts hung from their stalls with a huge picture of Vialli's face staring out from them looking gloomy. 'Cheer up Luca,' the legend read, 'you can play every week now'.

By the main gates leading towards the Shed, there was a little knot of people holding clipboards and seeking signatures. But they were not canvassing for Gullit or seeking redress for what had been done to him. They were protesting about significant rises in the cost of season tickets, something Gullit's pay demands would have exacerbated.

In general, the crowd seemed to be obeying the club's exhortations to get behind the new man. Much though Gullit had been loved in west London, the supporters were more concerned with the vanquishing of Arsenal and the prospect of a second trip to Wembley in consecutive seasons.

For Vialli, it was a real baptism of fire. Win and he was at Wembley with some breathing space to start getting things right; lose and the mutterings about the demise of Gullit were bound to increase and suddenly Chelsea would be looking at a season that was beginning to peter out. The stakes were higher than at any other Chelsea game all season.

In his musings in the matchday programme, Vialli tried to rally the fans and placate them over Gullit. 'Some of you might feel a little bit sad because of Rudi's departure,' he wrote. 'Some might worry that now we are achieving something, we shouldn't make such radical changes. Some might think I'm the wrong man for the job.

'But the real Chelsea supporter will never ever forget that whenever these decisions are taken, they are for the sake of the club, to ensure the future in the best way. If I'm the right person, we shall do better than before.'

Before the game, Vialli gathered his team together in the centre of the dressing room and poured them each a glass of champagne. Faustino Asprilla used to like a glass of wine before a Newcastle match but this was different. Vialli asked them to drink, to mark the beginning of something new, to drink in the beginning of his spell in charge. 'It was cheap stuff,' Mark Hughes said afterwards. 'It wasn't the sort of stuff you swill around in your mouth but then again it wasn't the sort of stuff you spit out either.'

Vialli answered the first question everybody had been asking by playing in the Chelsea attack, in an adventurous 4–3–3 formation he had grown used to at Juventus and which he was keen to try out on his managerial debut. Chelsea flung themselves at Arsenal like raging bulls and Hughes was lucky not to be sent off early in the first half for a series of lunges at Patrick Vieira.

But then Arsenal failed to clear a cross and as the ball bounced around in the box, Hughes reacted to it first and lashed it past Alex Manninger, the replacement for the injured David Seaman, to bring Chelsea level on aggregate. The stadium went wild. Then, early in the second half, came the defining moment of the match and possibly of Chelsea's whole season, the single incident that turned things Gianluca Vialli's way. He helped to fashion it, contesting a tackle on the right wing. Eventually, the ball found its way to Roberto Di Matteo and he scored with a shot of such venom and majesty that it rivalled his quickfire strike against Middlesbrough in the FA Cup Final at Wembley.

Sitting in the press box, I saw Vialli out of the corner of an eye in the second after the goal went in. He was sitting on his backside on the pitch by himself. The injury that he had sustained in a tackle was forgotten. He was facing away from the Arsenal goal with his legs stretched out in front of him, his fists clenched and his face contorted in an expression of such joy and relief that it seemed certain he had

A dramatic moment for Vialli during his first match in control, against Arsenal. He wins the ball, is brought down by a crunching tackle and is still grounded as Di Matteo scores one of the crucial goals that puts Chelsea through to the Coca-Cola Cup Final.

Vialli takes advice from his assistant manager, Rix.

Captain and manager celebrate as another trip to Wembley beckons.

never experienced anything like it before. That moment was the distillation of everything he had striven for in that first match, the catharsis that enabled Chelsea to begin the process of putting Gullit behind them. For me, it was the image of the season.

Dan Petrescu put things out of reach with a third goal and even though Dennis Bergkamp pulled one back with a penalty after Graham Rix had substituted Vialli late in the game, it was too late for Arsenal to spoil the Stamford Bridge celebrations. More than two hours after the final whistle had blown, the London-bound platform at Fulham Broadway was still thronged with deliriously, raucously happy Chelsea fans chanting one name. 'Vi-ar-lee,' they sang over and over again. 'Vi-ar-lee'.

THE NEXT DAY, VIALLI WAS AT HARLINGTON early, still trying to run up the learning curve. He wandered over to one of the pitches furthest from the pavilion to run his eye over the reserves, something that no one could remember Gullit doing. Gullit had made a virtue out of dealing only with the first team and in this he had been encouraged by Bates. Sitting on his plastic chair, outside the double doors, Rix watched Vialli watching the reserves. 'Luca,' he said. 'He'll never have a problem in life. You know why. Because he's a winner.'

The next Saturday, though, Vialli lost his first Premiership game, at Leicester City, then lost again at home to Manchester United courtesy of the only goal from Phil Neville, and suddenly it was not all plain sailing. Suddenly, with Zola struggling for form and fitness, Vialli discarded the 4–3–3 system he favoured and reverted to Gullit's rotation system. He even seemed to outdo Gullit by playing Dmitri Kharine in goal for league matches and Ed De Goey for the cup games. No matter, they lost away to Real Betis in the Cup Winners' Cup quarter final first leg,

too, before the Coca-Cola Cup came to the rescue again, this time in the shape of the final against Middlesbrough, their vanquished Cup Final opponents ten months earlier.

In the preamble to the game, which took place on a Sunday, 29 March, Vialli took a little time off from training to pose for the cameras with Wise and two giant caricatures of the two of them at Harlington. As he stood patiently outside for the photographers, Di Matteo was telling the media that the man he used to consider his friend had indeed begun to change with the new pressures he faced.

'He doesn't laugh as much as he did before,' Di Matteo said. 'Since Luca became manager, I have lost a friend. The relationship has changed. We don't go out together now. He has to think about everything now. As a player, he could switch off when he went home. Now he has to think about training the team, the players and everything. He's not joking as much in training now he's the manager. He has a lot of pressure and I feel for him. But he made the decision to take the job and now he has to take the pressure. We knew that would happen when he became the manager. I know I can't have Luca back as a friend now that he's the manager but it's very important to win the Coca-Cola Cup. Then maybe we can be friends again for one night.'

Vialli recognised it, too. 'It is true that I think about things too much,' he said, 'but it's getting better. I have to try to get some proper sleep in before this final, six or seven hours a night at least.'

So keen was he to prepare properly, though, and to stay in control during the match that he left himself out. Not just out of the starting line up either. He did not even give himself a place on the substitutes' bench. Instead, he walked proudly out of the Wembley tunnel at the head of his team, dressed in a suit.

Coca–Cola Cup Final Day: Chelsea fans converge on Wembley Stadium with hopes high.

A family outing for father, son and grandson sharing a special moment in their club's history.

Middlesbrough were not the easy touch they had been at the end of the previous season. Then, they had been exhausted by their fruitless fight against relegation from the Premiership and the internecine arguments that had torn their team apart. This time, they were riding high in the Nationwide League Division One, inspired by Paul Merson and buoyed by the fact that Paul Gascoigne would be making their first appearance for them since his move south from Glasgow Rangers. Gazza started on the bench.

The Chelsea fans began by taunting their Middlesbrough counterparts with chants of 'Can we play you every week' and sang lustily when the recently acquired club anthem 'We're going to make this a blue day' was played over the loudspeaker system. Out on the pitch, Di Matteo was resplendent in a pair of white boots made specially for the occasion.

After twenty-two minutes, Chelsea nearly drew first blood. Le Saux, who was denting Merson's attacking brio with his constant forays down the left, crossed from near the by-line and Hughes hit it fiercely on the half-volley and brought a fine save out Schwarzer. Fifteen minutes into the second half, Zola curled a shot against bar after a one-two with Petrescu. Then Gascoigne entered the fray.

Almost immediately, he was booked for a foul on Wise and almost in an instant the two of them seemed locked in their own private war. Gazza was booked for a foul on Wise, so Wise got booked for a foul on Gazza that nearly cut him in half at the knee. A few minutes after that, Gascoigne was lucky to stay on the pitch after he brought down Wise as he sprinted towards the Middlesbrough area.

As extra time beckoned, Oz, the kit man, arrived in front of the Chelsea bench with extra bottles of water and Gatorade. When the whistle went to signal the end of normal time, Vialli disappeared for a few seconds and then came racing back on to the pitch.

He spoke to every single player, exhorting them, encouraging them, willing them on.

Five minutes later, Chelsea were in the lead. Wise crossed from the by-line and Sinclair, who already had made two crucial defensive interceptions, rose above the Middlesbrough defence and guided his header downwards and past Schwarzer. Vialli was off the bench in an instant, punching the air. Three minutes from the end, Di Matteo turned in Zola's low corner at the near post and it was all over.

Then, even in the midst of their celebrations, the Chelsea players broke with tradition to show just how much they appreciated the sacrifice Vialli had made by not playing, to show how much respect and affection they had for their new manager. Instead of Wise going up the steps to receive the cup, the Chelsea captain held his team back and they sent Vialli up instead, suit and all.

So he climbed the steps, looking incongruous in that grey suit among all the blue shirts and the sweating brows and he took the cup in both hands, kissed it and held it up high above his head to the applause of the Chelsea fans. In the background, Bates was applauding, too, smiling broadly. Rarely can a vindication – even a superficial one – of a controversial managerial change have happened so quickly.

'I spoke to Steve Clarke before the game and told him what I intended to do,' Wise said. 'He agreed. At the final whistle, I told Luca the players wanted him to go up the steps first. He was clearly delighted and we are so pleased for him. This bloke is honest, straight with us and a nice fella. We appreciate him. That's why we want to win for him and why we told him to go and get the Cup. It was important Luca was part of this. It must have been hard for him to leave himself out of a Cup final.'

Vialli, of course, was happiness personified. 'It

Mark Hughes and Nigel Pearson battle for supremacy in the air.

A tense moment for Chelsea as Middlesbrough take a free-kick.

Paul Gasgoigne helps Dennis Wise off the ground after a clash between the two hard men.

In the stands Chelsea fans celebrate a well-earned victory while in the dressing room, Graham Le Saux admires Chelsea's new cup.

Dan Petrescu calls home with the news of victory.

was wonderful for me,' he said. 'One of the great moments of my career. I feel honoured and happy. It gave me so much satisfaction. It showed me the players care about their player-manager. I wanted to be involved of course. But there were only three subs and I had about ten players in the stand who also wanted to be part of this. We must also not forget Ruud Gullit tonight. He helped to get us to this Cup Final and I am sure he will be delighted we have won it.'

Before he walked off the Wembley pitch, he watched his players and his staff cavorting. Terry Byrne, the club's assistant physio, was dancing and swaying like a drunk, weighed down by a huge top hat. 'Glenn Hoddle told me to celebrate properly because you never know when you'll be in a Cup Final again,' he said. Then, when the Chelsea anthem began to play again, the whole team linked hands and ran as one towards their fans opposite the tunnel end and flung themselves to the floor.

Vialli simply walked over to the fans and bowed a simple bow. And in the morning, the headline on the back page of the *Sun* read 'Suits You Sir'. Vialli and management seemed to be taking to each other.

CHELSEA NOW HAD ANOTHER SEASON OF European competition in the Uefa Cup and it reassured supporters, players and directors that the momentum carrying the club forward since the days of Hoddle, which had been given tangible form by the triumph in the 1997 FA Cup Final, was still rolling forward. It was crucial not to let the feel-good factor that Gullit, in particular, had engendered among the supporters slip away, and this latest victory over Middlesbrough secured it for another season.

By now, though, Chelsea had fallen out of the race for the league title as Arsenal and Manchester United joined in the titanic struggle at the top. They had one final say in the make-up of the Premiership, on the last day, when goals from Vialli and Jody Morris consigned Bolton Wanderers to defeat at Stamford Bridge and a return to the Nationwide League. At Goodison Park, where Everton had only drawn with Coventry City but had been saved from the drop by Chelsea's victory, fans sang the Vi-ar-lee chant as they streamed out of the exits towards Stanley Park.

If Everton and Bolton Wanderers still had relegation to fret over until the final day, though, the only focus left for Chelsea after the Coca-Cola Cup, the only thing stopping their season from drifting away into anti-climax, was the pursuit of the European Cup Winners' Cup. After Real Betis were overhauled in the second leg of the quarter-final in the middle of March, Chelsea drew Vicenza of Serie A in the semi-finals.

In the first leg, at the small Communale Stadium on the outskirts of the beautiful Palladian city, Chelsea were over-cautious and lost to the only goal of the game from the lanky forward, Zauli. It could have been more and Chelsea hardly threatened an away goal. The mood on the plane home was glum. The feeling was that they were on their way out of the competition. That feeling intensified when Pasquale Luiso, a striker who had voiced his ambition to be transferred to Chelsea before the game, scored in the first half of the second leg, leaving Chelsea needing three goals to win. The home defence had been in such disarray for the goal that it seemed they were more likely to lose by three.

But then Chelsea staged one of the most stirring comebacks the competition has ever seen. Gustavo Poyet, starting his first match after a six-month lay-off with a knee injury, brought the scores level on the night just before half-time. Five minutes after

The bench erupts in celebration after Mark Hughes
scores the goal that takes Chelsea to the
Cup Winners' Cup Final.

The walking wounded: hero of the hour Mark Hughes returns to the dressing room nursing an injured jaw.

Chaos in the dressing room as victory sinks in.

half-time, Zola scored with a bullet header after Vialli's searching cross from the right to tie the aggregate scores. Then, twenty minutes from the end, with Chelsea beginning to run out of steam, Rix sent on Hughes, who took only six minutes to make the difference. He ran on to a long kick from De Goey and volleyed it across goal with his left foot and into the bottom right-hand corner. Cup medals seem to stick to Hughes like magnets to a fridge. The Cup Winners' Cup Final against VfB Stuttgart in Stockholm in May would be his 12th major final and his second in the competition. He won the first with Manchester United against Barcelona in 1991.

When the final whistle blew, Hughes was horizontal in the Vicenza half, felled by a stray Italian elbow. He had to be helped from the pitch and nearly fainted in the dressing room. It was almost subdued in there. Despite the heroics, despite everything, the job was not yet done.

TO COMPLETE IT, CHELSEA FLEW to Stockholm on 12 May to take part in their first European final since they beat the great Real Madrid in the same competition in 1971. This was their chance to put themselves on a par with the swashbucklers of those years, to ensure that Zola, Di Matteo and Wise could be mentioned in the same breath and with the same pride and reverence as Hudson, Osgood and Cooke.

They began their preparations by going straight from the airport to Rasunda Stadium, a modest arena with high, steep all-seater stands in a nondescript suburb of the Swedish capital. After they got off the coach, some of the players wandered out to inspect the dry, rutted pitch, others were co-opted into a shambolic press conference.

First to speak, and the one everyone wanted to talk to, was Zola, who was still fighting to shake off a hamstring problem that many had feared would rule him out of the match and ruin his chances of going to the World Cup with Italy.

As he spoke, we had no idea of the significance of his words. He had had an indifferent season by his own high standards. He had fallen from the plinth we had all placed him on after he won the Footballer of the Year award the year before and become, in the process, the most admired foreign player in the Premiership, the example everyone pointed to when they wanted to prove what a beneficial influence the imports had been on the indigenous players in our league. 'It means a lot to me to play tomorrow . . . It won't be a gamble if I play. It would be foolish to gamble now and I can't do it. I will train tonight and if it goes all right, then I will be available. I do not want to play tomorrow if I cannot be at my best. It would be great to finish the season with a big victory. It would change the season from a so-so season to a successful one.'

Eventually, Vialli took his turn on the stage, too, still wearing his Nino Cerruti club suit and a light grey pullover underneath it. Sweat was trickling in small drops off his forehead and he looked drawn and tense. He started by saying that he hoped that Zola would be fit but soon his thoughts wandered to wider horizons and the significance of the game in the club's development.

'It is one of the most important matches in the history of the club,' Vialli said. 'Chelsea played their last European final twenty-seven years ago and it is a great achievement for us to be here. We have had an excellent season but if we were to win this, it would make it an extraordinary one. Every year, Chelsea is improving and whether we win or lose, we will have no regrets.

'I hope this match is going to be like a celebration of a very important moment in the history of the club. So far, the build-up has been almost as exciting as when I played in the European Cup final for Juventus two years ago. Looking to the future, I hope we can keep improving and keep making steps forward. I think the future is even better than the present and to win the final tomorrow would give us great confidence for the future. It would make the name of the club even better known in Europe and it would give us confidence for the championship next season.'

It was light at 4 a.m. on the morning of the final and some of the players could not sleep. The sun shone brightly all day and while the journalists and supporters either took boat trips to some of the hundreds of islands that dot the approaches to Stockholm or settled themselves into bars, the players put the finishing touches to their game plan.

When we arrived at the stadium about two hours before the game, which kicked off at 8.45 pm local time, the team coach was outside the main entrance, cordoned off from the mass of supporters. We filed past it on the way to the media door and noticed that there was one man sitting on it alone: Vialli, head bowed, deep in thought. He looked as though he was wrestling with one last selection conundrum. It was clear this was the biggest test of his fledgling managerial career.

In the press box, all sorts of rumours were flying around. Le Saux was out, it was said, and Zola had not even been given a place on the bench. Before the team sheets had been handed out, Le Saux emerged from the tunnel still in his suit and walked slowly round the touchline to the other side, where the match preliminaries were to take place. It was clear that he, at least, had not made it.

Then, about half an hour before the kick-off, with the television producers getting jumpy because they wanted to broadcast the line-ups, the team sheets finally appeared. Zola was on the bench. It was

tactical, people were saying. Flo was playing instead, because the pitch would not have suited Zola's style.

Eventually, after multiple playing of 'We're going to make this a blue day' had worked the Chelsea sections of the crowd – and they were almost everywhere because the Germans had taken only 4,000 of their allocation – into a frenzy, the teams were led on to the pitch and over to the main stand, where Bates sat in the directors box and the Uefa anthem was played. Then it was time.

Despite their support, despite the flags that said 'Vialli for Pope', 'Brixton Chelsea', 'Stevenage Chelsea', 'Thanet Blues' and all the rest of the proud manifestations of allegiance that equate to the standards noble houses used to carry into battle, Chelsea began as though they were wracked by nerves. Di Matteo missed a good early chance when he pulled his left-foot shot wide, and the Chelsea defence almost cracked as soon as it came under pressure.

In the ninth minute, Duberry tried to slip a short pass forward to Wise but it was easily intercepted by Balakov. He played it forward to Akpoborie, the Nigerian forward, but he lost his nerve at the vital moment and instead of shooting when he was clean through he passed it square and the danger was over. Three minutes later, Clarke's miscued clearance split his own defence and freed Bobic. His volley from the edge of the area beat De Goey but whistled just wide of his right-hand post.

A nasty edge entered the game now, too. Duberry was left nursing a bloody nose after Bobic caught him in the face with an elbow, and Wise attempted to exact a measure of retribution by body-checking Balakov as he sprinted through the middle. Wise was booked for that; Duberry was lucky to escape without a caution after a scything tackle on Bobic.

In the nineteenth minute, Stuttgart wasted their best chance of the game. Another defensive mistake, this time from Leboeuf, gave the ball to Balakov, who bore down on De Goey and unleashed a fierce left-foot drive, but the goalkeeper got down smartly and managed to push it out. It was one of the game's two turning points.

Thereafter, Chelsea seemed to be in control. Poyet had a fierce volley beaten out by Wohlfahrt, Stuttgart's Austrian goalkeeper, and then, on the stroke of half-time, Wise's blistering volley bent just wide of a post after Di Matteo's free-kick had been only half cleared.

Throughout the second half, Zola had been prowling the touchline, warming up, glaring in turns at Rix and at the pitch. At one stage, I saw Rix motion to him. He seemed to be holding up three fingers as if to say 'Three minutes and then you're on'. A pained expression came over Zola's face and he shrugged in frustration. He made sure Rix had got the message.

The coach, though, was as good as his word. In the seventy-first minute, with the game sliding drearily towards extra time, the fourth official went to the half-way line and indicated with his electronic board that Flo was off and Zola on – to a resounding cheer from the Chelsea supporters.

He touched the ball once, a defensive block. A second time, a misplaced pass. Then, as Wise received the ball midway inside the Stuttgart half, Zola tricked his inexperienced marker, Yakin, into following him into a deep position and then suddenly spun away from him and made his run towards goal. Wise had spotted his manoeuvre and chipped a pass right into his path. Zola ran on to it and as Wohlfahrt rushed out, Zola smashed a right-foot half-volley over him. It was still rising when it bulged the roof of the net.

Zola had been on the pitch just seventeen seconds but his celebrations knew no bounds. He said afterwards that they must have looked horrible. He ran towards the Chelsea contingent behind the goal, lost in his elation, jabbing both his fingers forward in a macabre sort of dance until he was mobbed by his team-mates. Rix leapt off the bench in delight, revelling in his subsitution. The timing of a replacement does not get much better than that.

For the rest of the match, inevitably, Chelsea had to fight a frantic rearguard action as Stuttgart pushed for an equaliser. This time, in contrast to their vulnerability at the beginning of the game, Duberry, Leboeuf and Clarke stood firm and repelled everything that was thrown at them.

The pressure increased in the eighty-fourth minute when Petrescu was dismissed for a badly-timed tackle on Yakin, and in the dying minutes even Wohlfahrt joined in the Stuttgart attacks. In one break, Granville, replacement for Le Saux, scampered down the left wing unaware that the goal was at his mercy, that Wohlfahrt was stranded in the Chelsea half. By the time the penny dropped, the goalkeeper had recovered his ground.

As the game went deep into injury time, the Chelsea staff and substitutes stood in front of their dugout and put their arms around each other's shoulders to form a chain, a sort of mental cordon against Stuttgart scoring. And in the end, the release came, the whistle blew and they set off on their own private missions of celebration.

Rix wheeled round in a circle of his own, lost in his joy. Most of the others either hugged one another or made for the players still out on the pitch. Some Chelsea supporters had to be urged to go back to their seats after they mounted a mini-invasion. Then Wise led the players on to a stage that had been hastily assembled on the pitch and the real celebrations began.

First they paraded around the pitch with the cup. Then Vialli broke away from the main group with

Zola goes wild after scoring the winning goal.
He had been on the pitch just seventeen seconds.

Pure joy for Chelsea's players and fans as the club wins its first European trophy in twenty-seven years.

their jesters' hats and their scarves that the fans had thrown to them. He spat emphatically and then broke into a run, heading for the other end of the pitch. In the centre circle he did a cartwheel and then he stood in front of the supporters drinking in their applause.

Soon he was joined by the rest of the team and they set off in a long line, holding hands, back towards the other end. When they reached the penalty area, they flung themselves to the floor in unison in a celebration that has become another football trademark. Not content with that, they ran to the other end and repeated the effect. At Heathrow Airport, in the early hours of the next morning, Le Saux undid his suit jacket and showed me his white shirt. It was covered with grass stains of brilliant green.

By the time the on-pitch celebrations had finished, they looked like a group of men who have been on a long night. Shirts were ripped, some did not have shirts at all. Gary Staker clung to Vialli's shoulder, still congratulating him, and Terry Byrne wandered back down the tunnel clad only in the flag of St George.

On the half-way line, the players staged one last tribute to their supporters. They ushered the photographers a respectable distance away and then bowed in unison to the fans behind the goal as if they were bowing to Mecca. They turned round and repeated the action to the supporters at the other end, and then they left. Last off, still holding the trophy high above his head, was Zola. Even in the tumult, I could hear him from where I was, his voice raised in one continuous yell of delight that only disappeared when he was deep inside the tunnel.

'This morning when I found out I was not playing,' Zola said in another chaotic press conference afterwards, 'I was a little bit surprised because I have worked so hard in the last few days to get myself fit. I was disappointed, but when I came on, I turned my frustration into something positive. It was quite incredible for me when I scored. I could not control myself. I am sure my celebration looked quite horrible but when you think your dream is dying, it is wonderful to see it come alive again.'

For the rest of us, the game was pregnant with significance. It was only the third time, for instance, that an English club had won a European competition since our readmittance after the Heysel disaster. It also marked a welcome piece of revenge for England over Germany after semi-final defeats in the 1990 World Cup and the 1996 European Championships and Manchester United's defeat by Borussia Dortmund in the European Cup in 1997.

More than anything, though, it was Chelsea's night; the night when their plan to join the European élite, the plan that has taken shape in the developments of Chelsea Village, assumed a tangible form on the pitch.

If Chelsea do it right, that night in Stockholm will be a starting point, not a sign that they can sit back. As a competition, it did not boast sides of the highest quality although Chelsea beat the best that it contained. But as a springboard to greater things, it could be the perfect foundation. New players will have to be bought, the defence, in particular, will have to be improved, but the force is still with them.

'This is a great club with a great history,' Vialli said, 'but we must never be satisfied. If you get like that, you never win anything again. It is only a game but it is life and death to me and the day I find myself becoming satisfied is the day I hang up my boots and my coaching whistle. I cannot help getting tense, nervous and angry. I have learnt a great deal in a short time as a manager. I have made mistakes and when that happens, all you can do is try to learn from them and try not to make them next time. I am planning for next season already. That is my mentality. I cannot stop thinking about the future. We have proved that we are a great team in Europe and in the cups but it is the Premiership title that we want now. I just want to thank God for all of this, because I was born lucky.'

With Vialli at the helm, the unpredictability that eventually became the hallmark of Gullit's regime at Chelsea seems to be disappearing, gradually if not completely. After the victory in Stockholm, the mood among the players was that Gullit, like Kevin Keegan with Newcastle United, had taken the team as far as he could but that they were on the verge of a deep trough. Vialli's appointment pulled them back from the brink of that trough and seemed to infuse them with a new urgency.

'Chelsea is a big club now,' Rix said on the plane home. 'It is a big club and I don't think it was before. We have got to learn with the pressure of being a big club. We have got to look at those Arsenal boys, that back four who have been together for the last ten years. They have had untold pressure week in and week out and they have been able to handle it and that is what we have got to aim for.'

The future is so bright now that all at Chelsea would have to wear shades, if they did not already possess a designer pair. Someone such as Dennis Wise is needed to try to keep things in perspective. When he was asked what differences he had noticed now that Vialli was in charge, he mentioned only one. 'Frank Leboeuf's moved into our changing room at Harlington now,' he said. 'It's terrible.'